# 60
## THINGS
# GOD Said
## about SEX

# Other Titles
## by
# Lester Sumrall

# 60
## THINGS
## GOD Said
## about SEX

## Lester Sumrall

**W**

WHITAKER
HOUSE

---

## 60 THINGS GOD SAID ABOUT SEX

ISBN: 0-88368-770-4
Printed in the United States of America
© 1993 by Lester Sumrall Evangelical Association

Lester Sumrall Evangelical Association, Inc.
P.O. Box 12
South Bend, IN 46624
www.lesea.org

Whitaker House
30 Hunt Valley Circle
New Kensington, PA 15068
www.whitakerhouse.com

---

Library of Congress Cataloging-in-Publication Data

Sumrall, Lester Frank, 1913–
60 things God said about sex / by Lester Sumrall.
p. cm.
Includes bibliographical references.
ISBN 0-88368-770-4
1. Sex—Biblical teaching. 2. Sexual ethics. I. Title.
BS680.S5 S93 2002
241'.66—dc21
2002006169

3 4 5 6 7 8 9 10 11 12 13 / 11 10 09 08 07 06 05 04 03

# Contents

# Introduction

Our modern world is glutted with talk about sex. The entertainment media, commercial advertising, even our schools' textbooks are brimming over with it. Raucous voices chatter about sex nearly everywhere you go. It seems to be the favorite topic of conversation.

Much of the talk you hear is cold and factual, even clinical, because people are fascinated by the simple mechanics of sex. Some are eager to compare notes about sexual techniques. Others like to tell jokes with sexual overtones—jokes that arouse sexual desires or assume that the listener has a perverted view of sex. And quite a bit of the "sex talk" surrounding us isn't talk at all, but a series of subtle allusions to sex: a well-timed pause, a wink, or a furtive gesture.

Most of the people who like to talk about sex ridicule the secrecy of the Puritans or the Victorians; but ironically, they are just as secretive about sex themselves! They can only discuss sex in a cryptic, suggestive way because they don't really know (or can't express) what sex means to them. They haven't come to grips with the real purpose of sex.

They are still like awkward adolescents who giggle and blush when they think about the facts of life. Sad to say, many Christians are still at this stage.

And so sex has become the most discussed but least understood aspect of human life. I think it is fair to say that we at the end of the twentieth century are living in the Sexual Dark Ages. We hear more about sex than our parents or grandparents ever heard, but we understand much less. Why? Because we have forgotten the *raison d'etre* of sex, the reason it exists.

Imagine you were a jungle native who found a Cadillac airlifted into the Amazon for a TV commercial. You would talk with your friends about it from daylight to dark. You would touch its shiny finish and peer into its plush interior. You would develop a strange attachment to it, a mixture of both curiosity and fear. *But you would not know why it was there.* You would know just as little about Cadillacs as you ever did—even less, because you would have acquired some strange misconceptions in the meantime!

And so it is with sex. The average person talks sex, sees sex, thinks and dreams sex, but is totally ignorant of God's purpose for sex. And so we have a whole new constellation of "helping" professions that try to untangle the knot of America's confused sexual mores. Family lawyers wade through a morass of hotly contested divorce cases, many of them directly related to sexual problems. Psychiatrists' waiting rooms are full of people agonizing over sexual problems. Social workers offer birth-control devices and free abortions to teenage girls, and their telephones ring twenty-four hours a day.

All this agony, all this confusion, all this ignorant babbling about sex just breaks my heart. I find myself saying, "Lord, help me tell these people the truth about

# Introduction

sex." *Let me show them what your Word says about it. Open their eyes to the joy and fulfillment of sex as You meant it to be.*

Our country needs to hear what God says about sex. He has not changed His moral standards to suit a profligate generation. He has not changed His plan for men and women to find sexual happiness in marriage. God made us sexual creatures, and we ought to understand the pattern He intended for us to follow in our sexual relationships. God says, *"My people are destroyed for lack of knowledge"* (Hos. 4:6). Sex is a perfect example of the truth of this statement; we desperately need to seek God's purpose in this area of our lives.

God's Word includes an amazing abundance of information about sex. Nearly every book of the Bible mentions sex, either directly or indirectly. In the following pages, we will look at sixty key Scriptures concerning sex and sex-related morals. This study is by no means exhaustive, and I encourage you to dig into the Word to learn more of what God says about sex. But I hope you will be enlightened and challenged by the studies in this book, just as I found new insights by preparing them. I believe they can help you find a happier, more meaningful life.

—Lester Sumrall

# 1

# The Sex Drive

Sex should be used, but in its proper place and time,
according to God's plan. Within that plan the sexual
instinct is a good thing, a powerful source of life and
unity between two beings. Outside of God's plan, it
quickly becomes a means of division, a source of cruelty,
perversion, and death.

—Walter Trobisch[1]

The Bible is a book about sex. It is a book about
God's creation of humankind and His ongoing
relationship with us, touching every aspect of
our lives. It is a book about birth, growth, maturity,
and death; a book about love, hate, despair, and hope; a
book about hunger, pain, pleasure, and ecstasy—and a
book about sex.

The Bible talks honestly about the human sex drive.
In fact, it is more forthright and honest in describing
the sex drive than many of the so-called sex manuals
published in recent years. For example, take a look
at Judges 14:1–2. This passage describes how a young

Israelite named Samson visited the Philistine territory of Timnath. Notice what happened when Samson went back home. As soon as he met his mother and father, he said, *"I have seen a woman in Timnath of the daughters of the Philistines: now therefore get her for me to wife"* (v. 2).

Doesn't that sound familiar? A young man sees an attractive young woman and on first impulse he says, "I want her!"

It reminds me of the story about an old hermit and his son who lived far back in the mountains, away from any other human beings. The boy had never seen another person besides his father. Finally, the old hermit decided to take the boy into town on his birthday to give him his first taste of civilization. Walking down the street, they passed a couple of pretty girls and the boy said, "What in the world are those?"

The old hermit was caught off guard. "Er, uh...That's nothing, Son," he said. "Just a couple of geese."

The boy seemed to accept that explanation, so they went on.

The pair spent a full day browsing around town, visiting the different shops. Some of the places they stopped were the livery stables, the sawmill, and the blacksmith shop. At last they decided to head for home. But before they left, the old hermit said, "Son, I'd like to get you a birthday present. Did you see anything here that you'd like to have?"

"Sure!" the boy said. "I want a couple of geese!"

No matter who you are, no matter what your background is, something inside you draws you to the opposite sex. God made you that way. All of His creation is interrelated. All of His creatures have mates designed especially for them.

Consider the plant kingdom. Any farmer will tell you that plants must have male and female organs in order to reproduce. Unless the pollen touches the stamen, unless the sperm reaches the seed, the plant cannot reproduce itself and there will be no crop the next year.

Or consider the animal kingdom. For every male there is a female, and vice versa. When you find a peacock in the wild, you can expect to find a peahen nearby. When you find a lion, a lioness won't be far away. The two sexes live together, protect one another, and bring new life into the world. This is the pattern God established when He created the world.

The same is true of human beings. God created us as males and females, and He intended for us to be attracted to one another. God gave each person an endowment of physical forces—psychologists call them "drives"—that enable him or her to live and grow. One is the drive for *self-preservation,* the compulsion to protect oneself, find food for oneself, and find shelter from bad weather. Another is the drive for *religion,* a way to satisfy one's awareness of the spiritual realm. Yet another strong drive, and perhaps the one that is most misunderstood, is the human desire for *sex.* This is the compulsion to seek out and mate with a member of the opposite sex, to enjoy the physical pleasure of sex, and to produce offspring.

Many Christians believe that the sex drive is evil, so they attempt to repress or ignore it. Some even believe that sexual intercourse was the original sin. That idea deserves special attention, because it has affected the sexual behavior of Christian people for centuries.

St. Augustine, one of the great theologians of the early church, felt that sex was sinful. Augustine believed that the account of Adam and Eve's sin against God (see Genesis 3) uses symbolic language and that the "forbidden fruit" actually stands for sex. He thought that Eve conceived and bore children in pain (Gen. 3:16) because sex is sinful, and any kind of sexual activity brings pain. According to Augustine, human beings should ask God's forgiveness for even thinking about sex and abstain whenever possible. In fact, Augustine said, men and women who want to be righteous in God's sight should live in celibacy (that is, without any sexual contact); his adherents believed their leaders should live in church monasteries and convents, without even conversing with the opposite sex.

Augustine was a keen theologian, and his ideas were well-respected. His understanding of sex became a standard church doctrine, and we are still feeling the effects of his teaching. In his book on Western sexual morality, C. W. Lloyd says:

> Augustine's writings have probably exerted more influence in the West on love and sexual practice than those of any other man. The clearest expression of the innate evil in sexual passion, even within marriage, is set forth. These teachings...gave theological structure to feelings of guilt and shame in a biological drive. However, the enforcement of the doctrine of sexual guilt was difficult. The struggle to impose celibacy on the clergy...was only moderately successful until well into the Middle Ages.[2]

In other words, Christians had a hard time accepting Augustine's ideas about sex. They weren't certain that God wanted them to live in celibacy. The church had to struggle to keep its leaders obedient to this rule; in fact, the sexual prohibition was one of the first doctrines that Martin Luther and the other great Reformers broke away from. (Luther himself left a monastery to marry a nun.)

# The Sex Drive

Either Augustine was wrong, Luther was wrong, or both of them were terribly confused about sex. Was sex the original sin? Is the sex drive something evil? Notice what God says:

*1. So God created man in his own image, in the image of God created he him; male and female created he them. And God blessed them, and God said unto them, Be fruitful, and multiply, and replenish the earth....And God saw every thing that he had made, and, behold, it was very good.*
*(Gen. 1:27–28, 31)*

This passage indicates that the creation of man was very special in God's sight. God used His hands to make man (Gen. 2:7), which also manifests how important and precious we are to God. Everything else He created by giving His command: He spoke the stars into existence; He spoke the sun, the moon, and earth into existence; He spoke the plants and animals into existence. But He made man with His own hands, shaping him out of the dust of the ground. He breathed the breath of life into man's nostrils. He created a beautiful garden where man could live (Gen. 2:8). Obviously, God was pleased with the person He had made. He set out to make man in His own image, and He was satisfied with the results; He felt that man was "very good."

What else does the Bible tell us about this person whom God created *"in his own image"*? We learn that He created *two* people—people of opposite sexes. And right after God created the first man and woman, He told them, *"Be fruitful, and multiply, and replenish the earth."* God *commanded* the man and woman to have sexual relations with one another to bring children into the world. It would have been sinful for them *not* to have intercourse. They would have been disobeying a direct order from God if they had not conceived children through sex.

No other creature in the universe can bring another human being into existence. Angels cannot do it, animals cannot do it, no creature of any kind can do it—except man and woman. God gave us this special distinction. We are the only creatures who can bring into this world another creature with an immortal soul. We are God's partners in spiritual creation. Isn't that awesome? And it should impress us once again with God's divine purpose in giving human beings a sexual nature, a sex drive.

Never forget: The sex drive is God-given. You did not create your own sex drive. It was not made by TV, the movies, or dirty magazines. God made it! And God made it *"very good"*!

## Controlling the Sex Drive

Even though the sex drive is good, it must be controlled. This is true of any biological or psychological drive that God has given us. Imagine what would happen if you did not control the drive to eat. You would be eating constantly, indiscriminately. I've heard it jokingly said that some people "eat anything that doesn't eat them first"; well, if you didn't control your drive for food, that would literally be true. You would pile your plate high repeatedly, and you might even try to eat the plate itself. You would be obsessed with eating. Even though hunger is a healthy drive—a drive we must satisfy in order to survive—it can destroy us if we let it run out of control. The same is true of the sex drive.

Carnally-minded humanity would like to give free rein to the sex drive, as can be seen in much of society today. Nearly every town has a strip of massage parlors, peep shows, and brothels—where people go to indulge themselves sexually without inhibition or control. They would let their sex drive run wild day after day, twenty-four hours a day, if they could. One British writer wistfully concluded:

> It would be much easier if, like our monkey relatives, we...were more truly biologically promiscuous. Then we could extend and intensify our sexual activities with the same facility that we magnify our body-cleaning behaviour. Just as we harmlessly spend hours in the bathroom, visit masseurs, beauty parlours, hair dressers, Turkish baths, swimming pools, sauna baths, or Oriental bathhouses, so we could indulge in lengthy erotic escapades with anyone, at any time, without the slightest repercussions.[3]

God's Word condemns this kind of thinking. An uncontrolled physical drive will destroy the body. At first such indulgence may seem enjoyable; in the end, it will destroy you.

We will come back to this matter of promiscuity—letting the sex drive run uncontrolled—in a later chapter. For now let us consider why the sex drive should be controlled and how it can be controlled.

We have already seen that God says sex is a very beautiful and wholesome thing. He intended from the very beginning for us to have a sex drive. But He also tells us that the sex drive must be used for the purposes He intended:

> *2. If a man find a damsel that is a virgin, which is not betrothed, and lay hold on her, and lie with*

*her, and they be found; then the man that lay with her shall give unto the damsel's father fifty shekels of silver, and she shall be his wife; because he hath humbled her.* (Deut. 22:28–29)

Here God deals with sexual intercourse between two unmarried people who mutually agree to have intercourse. Today we hear some people say that "consenting adults" should be free to engage in any kind of sexual activity they want, even though they are not married; but God says no. Why? Because this kind of sexual relation "humbles" the woman. (The Revised Standard Version translates the word as "violated"; it would be just as accurate to say that the woman is "humiliated.") Her integrity is destroyed; her self-worth is cheapened by having sexual relations with a man who is not her husband and who refuses to become her husband. Such a man treats her as just another morsel for his sexual appetite. He does not love her; he loves the pleasure he gets from her. God says this is not what He expects a man and woman to do with their sex drives.

Dwight Hervey Small, a pastor and counselor who has taught for many years at Wheaton College, sheds more light on the problem:

> Sexual intercourse is an act which affects the whole personality, a personal encounter between a man and a woman in the depths of their being, which does something permanent to each, for good or for ill. Hence it cannot be treated merely as a sensual indulgence, the effects of which pass with the act.[4]

God intended sex to be this kind of personal encounter, a kind of interaction which is only proper in marriage.

# The Sex Drive

"But," someone may think, "Who's to say what is 'proper'? Why is intercourse in marriage the only 'proper' use of sex?" God made sex for the purpose of marriage; any other usage perverts this purpose. You can use a claw hammer to scrape ice off your sidewalk, but that's not the proper use of a claw hammer. The hammer wasn't made for scraping ice, and using it that way will ruin it for its intended purpose. The same is true of sex: There is one proper use of sex and many improper uses. God says we should control our sex drive for its proper use.

Realizing the proper use of sex is the first step toward controlling the sex drive. When you know how God wants you to use the sexuality He gave you, the goal is set. The standard is established. You then know that anything that undermines or hinders the proper use of your sexual powers should not be done; by the same token, anything that helps you fulfill or enrich the proper use of your sexual powers should be done. Like any other human drive, the sex drive can be trained and enhanced by new experiences and skill. You can learn techniques that will make your sexual relationship more enjoyable and rewarding, and in so doing you honor the Creator who gave you this wonderful ability we call "sex."

## The Sex Drive and the Total Person

As Reverend Small noted, sexual relations involve the total personality. We need to understand the full-orbed nature of the sex drive and how it interacts with other components of the personality. We need to appreciate the spiritual effects of the sex drive, as well as the physical effects. Otherwise we will be unable to control and utilize the sex drive to its utmost potential.

We might say that the sex drive functions in three worlds, or in three different planes of the human personality. In my book *Ecstasy*, I explain how each person is three-dimensional: Each person has a body, a soul, and a spirit.[5] These three components make up the whole person.

## Sex and the Body

We know, of course, that sex involves the *body*, the physical component of our being. A sexual relationship is the most intimate physical bond that can exist between two human beings, as a man and woman use their bodies to express their love and appreciation for one another. All five physical senses are involved:

—*Seeing* the physical charms of your loved one.

—*Hearing* your mate's words of endearment and desire.

—*Smelling* the scent or fragrance that uniquely belongs to your mate.

—*Tasting* the sweetness of each kiss.

—*Feeling* the caresses of your loved one's hands.

A sexual encounter is probably the most remarkable experience any person can enjoy on this earth, because it involves every aspect of the physical self. Howard and Charlotte Clinebell, a husband-and-wife team of Christian marriage counselors, have well expressed the physical joy that many couples have found:

> Sexual intimacy is more than the bringing together of sexual organs, more than the reciprocal sensual arousal of both partners, more even than mutual fulfillment in orgasm. It is the experience of sharing and self-abandon in the merging of two persons, expressed by the biblical phrase "to become one flesh."[6]

They are referring to one of the most candid statements God's Word ever made about sex. It comes just after the Bible tells us how God created woman as a "fit helper" for the man:

*3. Therefore shall a man leave his father and his mother, and shall cleave unto his wife: and they shall be one flesh.* (Gen. 2:24)

In other words, the physical tie of a man and woman through sex is even stronger than the physical tie of a child to his parent. The bond of sexual intimacy takes a higher priority than the affection you have for your father or mother. So far as God is concerned, a man and woman who enter into sexual union have become "one flesh"— they are one physical person. And if you must choose between honoring your parents or honoring your mate, God makes it crystal-clear that your mate comes first.

Many marriages fall apart because one or both mates fail to realize this! They are unwilling to put Mom or Dad in the proper place, below husband or wife. But God's Word says that a person who marries should leave his or her parents and set up housekeeping somewhere else. A house isn't big enough for two men, and it's not big enough for two women. If you want to have sexual relations with someone, you ought to get married; and if you are to get married, you ought to leave your parents and find a place of your own. That's the only way you can have physical intimacy.

## Sex and the Soul

The sex drive also involves the *soul*. Your soul is composed of your mind, emotions, and will; all three of these are affected by the sex drive.

The *mind* weighs everything that goes into decisions. It considers the facts; it measures the pros and cons; it evaluates your feelings. Some conscious decisions are made about your sexual desires; but sex influences many of your everyday decisions, whether you realize it or not. Your mind acts like a referee in the midst of your will, your emotions, your opinions, and many other competing influences—including your sex drive.

The *emotions* are very clearly affected by the sex drive. Sexual motives can cause a person to swing from one emotion to another. Perhaps you've seen your mate turn from happiness to disappointment, or even to anger, because of a sexual problem between the two of you. It can happen very easily, and you may not discern the reason for the sudden change. At a time like this, you need to have a heart-to-heart talk with your mate to learn what's behind his or her feelings.

The *will* is also strongly influenced by the sex drive. The will is your self-guidance system; it asserts what you want to do, regardless of what the mind may objectively tell you to do or what the emotions may try to sway you to do. The sex drive can persuade your will to desire sexual satisfaction.

These three components—the mind, the emotions, and the will—comprise the soul, the element of your nature that gives you your own unique identity. Your soul may be dedicated to God or it may be unregenerate and sinful. Either way, the sex drive influences your soul, and your soul directs how you will use your sex drive.

## Sex and the Spirit

You are also a spirit. God created your body and soul; but the God-breathed, eternal essence within you is your spirit. The spirit is the divine element that reminds your soul of God's will for your life. Your soul will be held accountable for the decisions it makes, for the Bible says, *"The soul that sinneth, it shall die"* (Ezek. 18:4). The spirit, though, does not die; it returns to God. (See Ecclesiastes 12:7.)

Is the spirit involved in sex? Yes! The ecstasy of your spirit, your consciousness of faith in God, and all the other aspects of your spirit are involved in the sex act. Your spirit can employ the sex drive to honor God—if your soul permits it.

## A Serious Matter

The sex drive, as we have seen, touches every component of the person. For that reason the sex drive must be handled with care and respect. If abused or allowed to have its own way, the sex drive can destroy you completely. It can not only debilitate your body, it can corrupt your soul and alienate your spirit. Our handling of the sex drive is a very serious matter.

I am afraid that our generation has played with the sex drive as if it were a toy. Men and women have pretended that the sex drive is just basic instinct that should be freely gratified, like the animals gratify theirs. This is a fallacy. The human soul is immortal, and anything that affects the soul should be taken seriously.

God has given us in His Word some very direct, explicit commands regarding sex. If we keep His commands, we will enjoy happy lives on this earth; we will have beautiful children and grandchildren; we will see generation after generation of our descendants cross the stage of human drama. If we ignore what God says about the sex drive, we place ourselves under

His judgment. He tells us what the penalties will be, and we must expect to pay them if we disobey. God's spiritual laws are just as immutable as His physical laws. You might jump off a cliff and say, "Look! I'm defying the law of gravity!" You will still fall. The same thing happens when you defy God's spiritual laws. It is not your opinion about sex that matters. It is not the opinion of a cheap novel or magazine that matters. Only God's law matters. You can either conform to His law and enjoy sex as He intended it to be enjoyed, or you can defy His law and bring suffering on yourself.

The sex drive is not dirty. The sex drive is not sinful. The sex drive is a precious gift from God, to be used for His glory and our enjoyment. We need to respect it, control it, and obey God's laws concerning it.

## Notes

1. Walter Trobisch, *I Loved a Girl* (New York: Harper and Row, 1965), p. 3.

2. C. W. Lloyd, *Human Reproduction and Sexual Behavior* (Philadelphia: Lea and Febiger, 1964).

3. Desmond Morris, *The Human Zoo* (New York: McGraw-Hill, 1969), p. 121.

4. Dwight Hervey Small, *Design for Christian Marriage* (Old Tappan, N.J.: Spire, 1971), pp. 92–93.

5. Lester Sumrall, *Ecstasy* (Nashville: Thomas Nelson, 1980), pp. 21–31.

6. Howard J. Clinebell and Charlotte H. Clinebell, *The Intimate Marriage* (New York: Harper and Row, 1970), p. 29.

# 2

# Why Is God So
# Protective about Sex?

*A Christian is one who can wait...Wait for the complete
union. By not waiting you will gain nothing and you
will lose much. I will put what you would lose into three
words: freedom, joy, and beauty.*

—Walter Trobisch[1]

Only God has the right to make a final statement
on anything. God is the only final authority,
the only One who can enforce His will in the
end. He has the final word because He had the first
word. He created this world and everything in it. He
created you and me. He is the Maker of our lives, so He
is the only One who can say how we should live them.
For this reason, what the Bible says about sex has an air
of finality, a tone of absolute authority.

If you know that God is the final authority about
sex, you won't get upset with His instructions. You will
know He is telling you the truth about sex. You will

realize that if you follow His rules, you will enjoy sex to the fullest as it was meant to be enjoyed.

Of course, human logic often leads us to different conclusions about sex. For example, logic would suggest that since a single person has a sexual nature just like a married person, a single person should engage in sexual relations. God's Word says *no*. Logic would indicate that if some persons enjoy physical, sexual contact with members of the same sex, they should be allowed to have that. God's Word says *no*. Logic would say that if a person can enjoy sexual intercourse with a marriage partner, that person could enjoy it just as much—maybe more—with someone else. Again God's Word says *no*.

We find that God often overrules our own reasoning in matters of sex. When He does, He's usually less permissive than we would be. His rules are much tighter than we would make them. He is much more protective than we are inclined to be.

Why is God so protective about sex? Why does He govern sex with such strictness and care?

## Societies' Restrictions

Even primitive societies that have never heard the gospel of Jesus Christ impose some limitations on sexual conduct. In fact, all known societies have regulated sex in some way, either with written laws or unwritten customs and taboos. This shows that we human beings know, deep down inside, that sex is a very important and serious matter.

I once attended a jungle wedding in Paraguay. The boy wore only a string around his waist and the girl had a waistband and a simple band across her breasts. Yet despite the crude simplicity of that occasion, they stood before a campfire with reverent solemnity and pledged to take one another as husband and wife. Their family and friends were witnesses. After they exchanged their vows, the boy and girl danced around the campfire while their friends laughed and cheered. Then the couple walked down a jungle path to the simple hut he had prepared for their honeymoon night. It was a very simple wedding without many of the formalities we know in America.

However informal in some ways, some customs were absolute. The villagers did not permit the boy to touch any girl except the one he planned to marry. This strict regulation protected the virginity of the girls and kept order.

In Muslim countries, every unmarried woman must wear a veil to conceal her beauty from any men she might meet in her village. The enjoyment of a woman's charms is a privilege reserved for her husband alone.

In ancient China, the parents of a boy chose his bride while he was still a child, but the youngsters were not allowed to see one another until their wedding day. Why? To preserve their sexual purity.

Anthropologists have found similar laws and customs in every known society, both ancient and modern. Many of these communities had never heard of God, and certainly had never read the Bible; yet they knew by instinct that they should safeguard the dignity of sex. They knew it should be protected and used for the right purpose—within marriage.

## God's Protective Rules

So you see, God is not being overly protective about sex. He wants us to be happy. He has established His regulations about sex to reserve sex for its best use, within the intimacy of marriage. Even the primitive tribesmen know that sex can be vulgarized and cheap-ened, and in their own way they try to protect their young people from the painful consequences of vulgar sex. So why shouldn't God, who created sex and knows more about it than anyone, be even more protective about it?

God's specific regulations about sex show what great care He takes to preserve sex for its proper use. In the following chapters, we will make a more thorough study of God's regulations for sex in marriage. For now let's consider God's law against adultery. This protec-tive law reveals why He is so concerned about our sex lives.

*4. Thou shalt not commit adultery.*

*(Exod. 20:14)*

That's all. Now that's simple, direct, and to the point. It's also very protective. God knew that sexual fidelity was so important that He devoted one of His Ten Commandments to it. He put sexual infidelity alongside murder and robbery as a crime so serious that He simply said, *"Thou shalt not."* He did not give any reason for His command, because the reason was self-evident. As a country farmer might say, "Anybody with a lick of sense ought to know that." Anyone with the slightest idea of what sex is all about, of how deep and intimate the sexual relationship is, should know that adultery is a crime. But because we're trying to understand why God is so protective, let's review the reasons for this law.

First, adultery is a crime because it destroys a sexual relationship. We've already suggested that such a rela-tionship is the most beautiful and meaningful bond that two human beings can have; it is a relationship of

# Why Is God So Protective about Sex?

full commitment to one another. The man and woman give themselves wholeheartedly to one another, holding nothing back. Nothing is "saved" for someone else. Their complete and total sharing explores all areas of intimacy. When one partner leaves to have sex with someone else, the relationship is destroyed. The "one flesh" is torn apart.

Dr. Charles L. Allen has counseled scores of married couples during his years as a pastor. Notice what he says about adultery:

> In marriage there are two things which must exist. First, a solid affection, a love for each other entirely different from the love for anyone else. Second, complete trust in each other. Adultery destroys both.[2]

He's right! Adultery destroys the trust and confidence that is the foundation of any marriage relationship, any sexual relationship. It is an act of betrayal, a way of pulling back your commitment to the person who has your all. It rips up your *covenant* with the human being who has shared more than anyone ever shared with you.

Second, adultery is a crime because it denies a person's God-given duty to raise children. In this day of popular birth-control devices and abortion, many people don't link sex with bearing children. Bringing children into the world is still God's primary purpose for sex!

> On this basis, the love relationship between man and woman cannot be regarded as "fleshly"; it is in the highest sense the fulfillment of God's purpose in creating men and women. In entering this relationship, Christians are committing

themselves to their part in fulfilling the plan of God for mankind....It is a sign of commitment before God and an affirmation that this couple views its relationship as a part of God's will for his people.[3]

God gave man and woman a duty with the gift of sex; He commanded them to "be fruitful." If one mate decides to find sexual enjoyment elsewhere, he is ignoring the duty that came with his gift.

Third, adultery is a crime because it perverts the spiritual truth that sex symbolizes. God's Word compares the sexual bond between a man and a woman to the spiritual bond between Christ and His church. Read the following statement along with God's command in Exodus 20:14 if you want to understand why adultery is so sinful in God's sight:

*5. For the husband is the head of the wife, even as Christ is the head of the church: and he is the saviour of the body. Therefore as the church is subject unto Christ, so let the wives be to their own husbands in every thing. Husbands, love your wives, even as Christ also loved the church, and gave himself for it....For this cause shall a man leave his father and mother, and shall be joined unto his wife, and they two shall be one flesh. This is a great mystery: but I speak concerning Christ and the church. Nevertheless let every one of you in particular so love his wife even as himself; and the wife see that she reverence her husband.   (Eph. 5:23–25, 31–33)*

Adultery shouts to the world that Christ is going to turn His back on the church, or that the church is going to "fall in love" with someone besides Christ. That's heresy! A barefaced lie! Yet that's exactly what adultery is saying. It is a theological statement.

The poet Walter A. Kortrey expressed the cynicism of a non-Christian world when he said:

> If loving God
> Is nothing like
> The love I have for her—
> Then you can have it. [4]

But God says His love for us is *exactly* like the love of a man and woman. A man and woman sharing the joys of nuptial sex portray the love of Christ and His church. They demonstrate how Christ and the church give themselves completely to one another. Sexual love is a holy symbol.

True, only Christians realize this; but any couple that breaks up to find other sexual partners is blaspheming the truth of God's love. To put it bluntly, they act as if Jesus were a gigolo or the church a prostitute. The very idea is repulsive.

Do you begin to see why God is so protective about sex? He is interested in the physical happiness of men and women, but He's also interested in guarding spiritual truth. He knows that sex enters both planes—the physical and the spiritual.

We find this again in the prophecies of Ezekiel. Here God puts a spiritual truth into sexual language; He calls the disobedient city of Jerusalem a "harlot." As He describes what He will do to Jerusalem, we see His protectiveness toward His people's spiritual life as well as their sexual life. His treatment of the spiritual harlot, Jerusalem, gives us an inkling of how a physical harlot will be treated:

*6. And say, Thus saith the Lord GOD unto Jerusalem...When I passed by thee, and looked upon thee, behold, thy time was the time of love; and I spread my skirt over thee, and covered thy nakedness: yea, I sware unto thee, and entered into a covenant with thee, saith the Lord GOD, and thou becamest mine....But thou didst trust in thine own beauty, and playedst the harlot because of thy renown, and pouredst out thy fornications on every one that passed by; his it was....And I will judge thee, as women that break wedlock and shed blood are judged; and I will give thee blood in fury and jealousy.    (Ezek. 16:3, 8, 15, 38)*

God says that a woman who breaks wedlock is judged like a woman who sheds blood. An adulteress is just as bad as a murderess; both of them must pay with their lives. This is what He means when He said, *"I will give thee blood."* We will see in a later chapter that the penalty for adultery in Old Testament times indeed was death. We will also see that the adulterer still dies in other, less obvious ways. One should notice, though, how God describes adultery in such clear, graphic terms.

Read the entire sixteenth chapter of Ezekiel and you will get the full picture. There God punishes infidelity, whether it's spiritual or sexual. He just won't allow it, because He knows the consequences. Infidelity will destroy the person who does it, pervert the other persons involved, and make a mockery of God Himself. So God said, *"I will judge you* [spiritual harlots] *as women who break wedlock and shed blood are judged"* (Ezek. 16:38 RSV).

# Why Is God So Protective about Sex?

## A Christian's Concern

Our spiritual welfare and our physical welfare are equally important to God. He loves us and cares about us, so He's keenly concerned about both aspects of our lives.

We Christians need to realize this, because we often are so concerned about another person's spiritual life that we ignore the physical life. When we counsel with someone, let's not tune out any clues of sexual trouble. God cares about His people's sex life, and so should we.

Pastor Tim LaHaye tells of a friend who was holding evangelistic services in a certain city and staying with a fine Christian couple who were leaders in the local church. After breakfast one morning, the evangelist casually asked his hostess, "How are things going?" She broke down in tears. Her husband was a very aggressive man, she said, and in their sexual contacts he moved too fast. She did not really enjoy their relationship, but she submitted to him out of love. She asked the evangelist to pray that God would help them. Pastor LaHaye tells what happened:

> That night as he was getting ready for bed, the minister stepped into the bathroom to brush his teeth. Since the bathroom was between the two bedrooms, without trying to eavesdrop he could clearly hear his friend perform what he called "making love to my wife." It was all over in three minutes! It was nothing more than physical satisfaction of the masculine mating urge.
>
> The next morning the evangelist asked his friend to stay home from work, and they talked in the backyard for two hours. To his amazement,

this college graduate who dearly loved his wife didn't even know anything was wrong. Neither of these young people had read a book on the subject of sex and they had never been given marriage counseling. When the preacher finished the long-overdue counseling session, the young man was heartbroken. He confessed his selfishness to God and asked for divine wisdom in being the kind of husband that God wanted him to be.[5]

Yes, God is very protective about sex. It is a wonderful gift that we should also cherish and protect.

# The Sanctity of Human Life

Sex is important because human life itself is important to God. Human life is holy in God's sight.

"Alright," you may say, "but doesn't the Bible tell us that the human heart is *'deceitful above all things, and desperately wicked'* (Jer. 17:9)?" Indeed it does, and carnal man is a corrupt and despicable creature. But God does not want us to be like that. He created us in His own image, as a reflection of His own divine nature. And even though man has fallen from grace and lives under God's condemnation, each person still has the capacity for pure and holy living. Each person's life is priceless in the eyes of God. Speaking through the apostle Paul, God said:

*7. Do you not know that you are the temple of God and that the Spirit of God dwells in you? If anyone defiles the temple of God, God will destroy him. For the temple of God is holy, which temple you are.* (1 Cor. 3:16–17 NKJV)

# Why Is God So Protective about Sex?

This applies to sex as well as to any other aspect of our physical lives. We are not free to do as we please with our bodies; they are dedicated to God. Each one of us has a spirit, a divine element within us. We should handle our bodies in a way that will honor the spirit within, bringing glory to the God who made us.

You probably have seen pictures of the temple ruins of Greece. The Parthenon and other great buildings of the classical age are now crumbling. Their twisted columns lie scattered about the city of Athens like a child's broken toys. Once they were tall and beautiful, their polished marble arches shimmering in the afternoon sun. Centuries of war and riots and vandalism have left them a rubble. The "temples" of peoples bodies can be just like that. God intends for them to be strong and beautiful for His sake; but if we neglect or abuse them, they will bring honor to no one.

When God created Adam and Eve, He made their bodies pure, holy, and clean. He gave them their own unique sexual powers and brought them together into the intimate relationship of marriage. Their bodies were holy, their sex drive was holy, and their marriage was holy.

God warned them not to violate His commands, which reflected His own moral nature; yet they disobeyed Him and were banished from the Garden of Eden. Their souls became rebellious and corrupt. They passed that corruption on to their descendants, but that did not make their *bodies* corrupt! It did not make the sex drive corrupt. Granted, the descendants of Adam and Eve made corrupt use of their bodies—the generations leading up to the Flood were full of unspeakable immorality. Yet the human body itself did not change. It could still be used for holy or unholy purposes, whichever a person chose.

Several years ago, a major network staged a radio drama called "The Cartwheel." It was about the career of a silver dollar (back then they were so big that people called them "cartwheels"). The drama showed how this coin passed through the hands of first one person, then another, until it had been used by almost every type of character you could imagine. A bridegroom used it to pay for his honeymoon suite. (You can tell this was back in the 1930s!) A faithful parishioner dropped it in the offering plate at church. A gambler used it to bet on a crap game. A drunkard used it to buy a pint of whiskey. On and on it went. Obviously, the cartwheel could be used for almost any purpose, depending on its owner's inclination.

The same is true of the body. God created it to be a holy, wholesome thing. He created it to bring honor to Him. He has given us many guidelines to help us preserve and strengthen every function of the body—including the sexual function. Yet we alone decide what to do with it.

God knows everything about sex, and He intended for us to be very careful about how it's used. His rules for sex are very protective. Shouldn't we heed these rules?

## Notes

1. Walter Trobisch, *I Loved a Girl* (New York: Harper and Row, 1965), p. 87.

2. Charles L. Allen, *God's Psychiatry* (Old Tappan, N.J.: Family Library, 1974), p. 69.

3. Howard Clark Kee, *Making Ethical Decisions* (Philadelphia: Westminster Press, 1957), pp. 36–37.

4. Walter A. Kortrey, "Agape and Eros," *The Christian Century*, July 18, 1973, p. 749. Reprinted by permission.

5. Tim LaHaye, *How to Be Happy Though Married* (Wheaton, Ill.: Tyndale House, 1968), p. 72.

# 3

# Sex in Marriage (Where Else?)

[Marriage] was a divine plan and a God-given provision
for His creature—man. He who would corrupt this union
is guilty of affront to God, and he who despises the
relationship despises God who gave it.

—Paul Wilson[1]

Did you ever stop to think that the first two
people in the world were married? Today we
hear a great deal about the single lifestyle;
many people think it's more fun to be single than to
be married. But this was not God's original plan. After
God created Adam, He said:

> 8. It is not good that the man should be alone;
> I will make him an help meet for him.
>
> (Gen. 2:18)

39

The term *"help meet"* literally means "an appropriate partner." The Revised Standard Version says *"a helper fit for him."* In other words, God was a matchmaker. He made a woman who would be just what the man needed, and then He brought them together. They became lifelong mates and raised the very first family in the world, without the help of any marriage counselors or self-help books or even "Dear Abby." God matched them very well. In what ways was Eve "meet" or "fit" for Adam?

It seems clear that she was a good helper in the manual labor that Adam had to perform; after they left Eden, she became the very first farmer's wife, and that's not an easy job. I can imagine her making their clothes, foraging for firewood, threshing and storing the field crops that Adam brought in. No one had ever done this type of work before, but Eve seemed well suited to the task.

Also, she was a fit companion and adviser. She did not always give Adam good advice, but she did try to help him make decisions. She weighed theological questions in her mind, such as whether they should obey God's commands "to the letter," or follow the serpent's interpretation. She tried to steer Adam in the most sensible, reasonable direction. We would have to say that she was well matched to Adam in intellect.

She was also a fit partner in her sexual role. Her female charms were a perfect match to Adam's male features. She opened up a whole new realm of physical pleasure that Adam could not have known if he had spent the rest of his life alone. She was well matched to Adam in the sexual sense.

In every way, the first marriage brought together two people who needed each other. It mated two individuals whose lives would have been limited and lacking had they not been married. Adam and Eve had a successful marriage, even though they were failures in other respects. One important reason for this success was the fact that they were well matched sexually.

With the couples I counsel for marriage, the question of compatibility always comes up. The young man and woman want to know, "Are we right for each other?" So we talk about the things that ought to matter in a marriage, to see whether they "match up."

First of all, we talk about their spiritual life—Are both of them Christians? If not, do they realize the problems caused by being *"unequally yoked together"* (2 Cor. 6:14)?

We talk about their life's work—Do they know each other's plans for the future? (You'd be surprised how many engaged couples don't know!)

We also talk about sex—Are they attracted to one another sexually? Do they see in one another the physical qualities they think they will enjoy? Have they talked about the purpose of sex and the proper role of sex?

Many times they haven't. Christian couples are especially prone to think that if they're well matched in every other way, their sex life will just naturally fall in line. They don't talk about it. They don't think about it. And after they're married they get a rude awakening.

This doesn't mean that partners-to-be must be in perfect agreement about everything. In fact, I don't think that is ever the case. My wife and I have enjoyed a wonderful marriage for the past thirty-five years, but I still can't say that we're in total agreement about everything. We *complement* one another. The strengths of one offset the weaknesses of the other. I believe that should be true in every married couple's life.

A prospective husband and wife can save themselves a lot of unnecessary grief if they will have an honest, straightforward talk about what they expect from their relationship. The range of subjects most certainly must include the sexual aspect. Pastor Tim LaHaye says:

> Physical adjustment in marriage can be properly compared to the instrumental adjustment necessary for an orchestra to produce a beautiful, harmonious symphony. Contrary to popular opinion, "doing what comes naturally" does not automatically guarantee physical harmony in the marriage relationship.[2]

In other words, you may not *seem* like a perfect match sexually. But can you make the adjustments necessary? Are you willing to be patient with your spouse while you learn to satisfy each other's needs? A computer dating service will never be able to tell you this kind of thing: You must learn from each other how flexible you are—learn by praying about it and talking honestly about it *before* you marry.

## Sex Expresses Love

Perhaps no word in the English language is so misunderstood as the word "love." A secretary turns to her friend in the elevator and says, "Oh, Myrtle! I just love your new outfit!" A prizefighter scowls at his opponent and says, "I'd love to punch you in the mouth!" Starry-eyed young girls sigh and say, "I'm in love!"

What does "love" mean anyway? Particularly, what kind of "love" is married love? John Powell, a well-known Roman Catholic writer, says this:

# Sex in Marriage (Where Else?)

The young man who professes to love a young woman may often be deceived in thinking that the gratification of his own egotistical urges really constitutes love. The young woman who finds the voids of her own loneliness filled by the companionship and attention of a young man may well mistake this emotional satisfaction for love....The critical question always remains that of self-forgetfulness. Does the young man or woman...really forget himself and his own convenience and emotional satisfaction, to seek only the happiness and fulfillment of the beloved?[3]

That's a pretty tough standard, isn't it? Everyone likes to think of his own needs and wants; everyone takes for granted that "happiness" is a matter of satisfying those needs and wants. But true love forces you to go beyond yourself. It makes you think about the needs and wants of someone else. More important, it may cause you to sacrifice your own comfort and pleasure to give enjoyment to the one you love.

God's Word gives us a beautiful description of love, and it's one of the most important things God has ever said about sex:

> *9. Love suffers long and is kind; love does not envy; love does not parade itself, is not puffed up; does not behave rudely, does not seek its own, is not provoked, thinks no evil; does not rejoice in iniquity, but rejoices in the truth; bears all things, believes all things, hopes all things, endures all things.* (1 Cor. 13:4–7 NKJV)

Here is the perfect description of the role of sex within marriage. Your sexual relationship should express this kind of pure and selfless love for your mate. Otherwise you've missed the mark.

"But wait a minute, Dr. Sumrall!" someone may say. "I thought you told us that sex was for bearing children." Yes, that is the primary reason God gave us our sexual nature. But He also expects us to use sex to express our love for our mate. His Word says:

> *10. Let the husband render to his wife the affection due her, and likewise also the wife to her husband. The wife does not have authority over her own body, but the husband does. And likewise the husband does not have authority over his own body, but the wife does.*
>
> *(1 Cor. 7:3–4 NKJV)*

A married couple should have sexual relations, not just to conceive children, but to show one another their complete love and devotion.

Marriage is the most unique relationship on earth. It is above all other human relationships. Only in marriage do two people share their minds, their souls, and even their bodies. Only in marriage do two people pledge their lifelong loyalty, "forsaking all others," as the wedding vow says. Only in marriage do two people join with God to bring other human beings into this world—others who are created in the image of God.

Married love is holy because God created the marriage bond. He authorized the first wedding, and He is the only One who can rightfully authorize a wedding today. This is why Christian marriages should not be performed in some court clerk's office, on a judge's back porch, or in the couple's favorite social spot. The marriage is not designed to honor the state or honor the couple; it is designed to honor God. It should express the unselfish love that only God can give. So the wedding should be performed where God is publicly worshipped, asking God to sanctify it. God should be invited to "tie the knot" that no one can untie.

# Sex Is a Dialogue

Marriage is a lifelong conversation. It's an exchange of ideas, a sharing of joy and sorrow. When a man and woman pledge to "cleave only" to one another, that wedding vow means they will share their innermost thoughts and feelings with one another. They will communicate. Or to put it in a spiritual context, they will *commune* with one another.

*11. Nevertheless neither is the man without the woman, neither the woman without the man, in the Lord. For as the woman is of the man, even so is the man also by the woman; but all things of God.* (1 Cor. 11:11–12)

Here the Word of God reminds us that man and woman are physically tied to one another, all the way back to Creation. The woman was created from a rib that God took from man's side; the man has been born of woman, ever since Eve. Man and woman are intimately related; they are incomplete without one another. It is foolish to think that marriage is simply a partnership of two self-willed, independent people.

Husband and wife must share their total lives, and the sexual relationship is an important way of sharing. It demonstrates in a literal, physical way that they are one. It is a kind of physical dialogue. The Reverend Small says:

Dialogue takes place when two people communicate the full meaning of their lives to one another, when they participate in each other's lives in the most meaningful ways in which they are capable.[4]

That's a good description of the sexual relationship. It is a way of participating fully in another person's life without fear or selfishness. It is true dialogue.

Like any other kind of dialogue, the sexual relationship must observe certain courtesies. If you were having a conversation with another person, would you insist on "being in charge"? Would you refuse to hear what the other person says? Would you turn and walk away when you're through, regardless of whether the other person is still speaking? Of course not. That would not really be a "conversation." The same is true of the sexual relationship. Each partner must be sensitive to the other's needs, ready to respond, patient in letting the other express himself (or herself). Howard and Charlotte Clinebell describe a typical situation in which sexual dialogue breaks down. We might call it a sexual "communication gap":

It is important for the husband to understand that his wife literally can't respond as she and he would like, when her feelings are hurt, the bedroom is cluttered, or the children are stirring in the next room. It is well worth the effort to create the needed atmosphere to allow her romantic side to flower. Many women experience sexual arousal more slowly than their husbands and respond to considerable tenderness, caressing, fondling, and reassurances of love in the full enjoyment of intercourse.[5]

# Sex in Marriage (Where Else?)

So many couples become frustrated by their sexual differences and seek relations with others, instead of learning how to truly commune with one another. This kind of adjustment is a natural part of becoming a mature person. It is a part of learning to love. God says:

> 12. *Drink waters out of thine own cistern, and running waters out of thine own well....Let thy fountain be blessed: and rejoice with the wife of thy youth. Let her be as the loving hind and pleasant roe; let her breasts satisfy thee at all times; and be thou ravished always with her love.*
> (Prov. 5:15, 18–19)

I firmly believe that the men and women of America would have much more enjoyable sex lives if they would take time to learn how to really communicate in marriage, rather than "shopping around" for better sex mates. A man who patiently learns the sexual language of his wife will always be ravished with her love. The woman who tunes her ear to her husband's sexual messages will be fully satisfied. But it takes time. It takes patience.

Several years ago, Charlie Shedd wrote a series of letters to his young son-in-law to be, and they have become a classic in the Christian literature about sex. One of Dr. Shedd's most startling statements was that a husband and wife may need a "twenty-year warm-up" to learn real sexual enjoyment together. He said:

> Freedom to express your desires is a great goal, but, for the first twenty years,...it's more goal than reality.[6]

Many couples will be able to establish the lines of sexual communication much sooner than that, but it's still good advice. Husband and wife need to be patient in their sexual dialogue, even if it takes years to learn how to communicate.

## Sex Brings Pleasure

The carnal world would have us believe that pleasure is the *only* purpose of sex. Some prudish Christians think that pleasure has *nothing* to do with sex. Both are wrong. The sexual relationship is a very pleasurable one, and it should bring a great deal of enjoyment to a marriage. But we need to get the pleasurable aspect of sex in proper perspective, according to God's Word.

The entire Song of Solomon describes the pleasures of sexual love. Some critics say the Song of Solomon is an erotic book that has no place in the Bible; but they obviously don't know what "erotic" means. It comes from the Greek word *eros,* which means "love for the sake of physical pleasure." The Song of Solomon certainly describes physical pleasure, but no one can say that it depicts pleasure as the "be all and end all" of sex. This book shows that sex expresses the great love a husband and wife have for one another. In fact, many Bible scholars believe it is a symbolic picture of God's love for His people, the love of Christ for His church. No matter how one interprets it—literally (concerning marriage) or symbolically (concerning God)—we would have to say that the Song of Solomon puts sex and pleasure in proper perspective.

Let us look at just a couple of passages from this remarkable book:

## Sex in Marriage (Where Else?)

*13. Tell me, O thou whom my soul loveth, where thou feedest, where thou makest thy flock to rest at noon: for why should I be as one that turneth aside by the flocks of thy companions?*
*(Song 1:7)*

This is the bride's earnest plea to her groom. It underscores the message we have already heard from God, that a married couple should not seek pleasure with other companions. Here God puts His words in the mouth of the bride herself. She says, in effect, "Show me how I can find pleasure with you, darling. For why should I try to find it with your friends?"

I told you the Bible was very straightforward about sex, didn't I?

Read on in the Song of Solomon, and you will find the bride pleading with her husband again and again, begging him to find his sexual pleasure with her. Remember that this book was inspired by God, just like any other book of the Bible. We should watch for what He is teaching us about sex here. The bride says:

*14. Let my beloved come into his garden, and eat his pleasant fruits....I am my beloved's, and my beloved is mine: he feedeth among the lilies....I am my beloved's, and his desire is toward me.*
*(Song 4:16; 6:3; 7:10)*

See how the theme of pleasure runs throughout this book? Yet it is always pleasure as an expression of *love,* not just pleasure for its own sake.

In the first statement (Song 4:16), the bride invites her husband to *"eat his pleasant fruits."* This is a vivid and beautiful way of inviting him to enjoy the physical pleasures of her marriage bed. She then says that *"he feedeth among the lilies"* (Song 6:3). The lily is a symbol of purity or, in this case, virginity. The bride is happy to say that her husband is the only one who has tasted her sexual pleasures. She has saved them all for him, for she knew she would belong to him—and he to her! She says, *"His desire is toward me"* (Song 7:10). Any woman would like to say this about her husband. Despite all the other women whose physical charms might tempt him, *"his desire is toward me."* He finds his pleasure in the right place, with his wife.

Unfortunately, many Christians think that sex is a dull, mechanical sort of thing. They look on it as a duty, an obligation they have to their mate—like washing the dishes or mowing the yard. But sex is a pleasure! Sex is enjoyable! God intended sex for the mutual pleasure of husband and wife, and they should feel no qualms about exploring the many "treats" it holds for them. Tim LaHaye advises wives:

> Rid your mind of any preconceived prejudices or "old wives' tales" that tend to make you fear the act of marriage—or look on it as evil. Just because your mother or some other woman was not well-adjusted in the physical area of marriage is no reason you have to perpetuate her mistakes and resultant misery. Approach the act of marriage with pleasurable anticipation. God meant it to be good![7]

No kind of sexual pleasure is "off limits" to husband and wife, so long as it honors God. Some people think that only one particular technique of lovemaking is "holy," and all others are sinful; but you won't find that teaching in Scripture:

## Sex in Marriage (Where Else?)

*15. Marriage is honorable among all, and the bed undefiled; but fornicators and adulterers God will judge.* (Heb. 13:4 NKJV)

In other words, marriage is an honorable way for anyone to enjoy sex. Some other way—whether sex before marriage (fornication) or sex with someone else during marriage (adultery)—is condemned by God. Moreover, the marriage bed is "undefiled." There is nothing sinful about sex in the marriage bed; there are no taboos to observe with your partner. You need only observe the courtesies of dialogue and the dignity that any divine gift deserves.

# Sex Honors God

Before we leave the subject of sex in marriage, we should consider how the sex life of a Christian man and woman can bring honor to God. This is another important function of sex. God says that everything we do should honor Him:

*16. Therefore, whether you eat or drink, or whatever you do, do all to the glory of God.* (1 Cor. 10:31 NKJV)

Everything that we do—eating, sleeping, talking with our friends, conducting business, even sexual intercourse—everything should be done in a way that will glorify the Lord. He made us and He expresses Himself through us. As Paul said, *"It is no longer I who live, but Christ who lives in me; and the life I now live in the flesh I live by faith in the Son of God, who loved me and gave himself for me"* (Gal. 2:20 RSV). Thus every physical act of the Christian should express love for the Lord. This is the final test for the Christian's sex life: Does it honor the Lord?

If a man and woman share the joy of sex in marriage as the Lord intended, and if they regard one another with the love and respect that any Christian should have for another, their sex life will be a tribute to the Lord. But if they flirt with sex outside of marriage, they have broken His command. If they desire sexual relations simply for the thrill or physical "charge" they get out of it, with no thought of mutual love, they have cheapened it. Most sex manuals would tell us that the *method* of sex is all-important, but God's Word tells us that the *motive* is just as important. If a man and woman engage in sex with selfish or perverted motives, they waste one of God's most precious gifts. They insult Him. And they will have to pay the consequences. Dwight Small says:

> The distinctive thing about the Christian concept of sex is in thus fully acknowledging it as a biological function in man, but at the same time insisting that it is a function of the total personality which at its highest is spiritual. Its physical aspects cannot be disassociated from its spiritual aspects.[8]

This is the key. Sex cannot be understood apart from all the other aspects of a Christian's consecrated life.

In marriage, sex is a normal part of daily life, just as eating or any other physical function. So we should not be reluctant to talk about it. We should thank God for sex and strive to use it as joyously and reverently as any other gift from Him.

# Notes

1. Paul Wilson, *The Institution of Marriage* (Oak Park, Ill.: Bible Truth, 1969), p. 8.

2. Tim LaHaye, *How to Be Happy Though Married* (Wheaton, Ill.: Tyndale House, 1968), p. 53.

3. John Powell, *Why Am I Afraid to Love?* rev. ed. (Chicago: Argus Communications, 1972), pp. 19–20.

4. Dwight Hervey Small, *After You've Said I Do* (Old Tappan, N.J.: Revell, 1968), p. 51.

5. Howard J. Clinebell and Charlotte H. Clinebell, *The Intimate Marriage* (New York: Harper and Row, 1970), p. 145.

6. Charlie W. Shedd, *Letters to Philip* (Old Tappan, N.J.: Spire, 1968), p. 110.

7. Tim LaHaye, *How to Be Happy*, p. 68.

8. Dwight Hervey Small, *Design for Christian Marriage* (Old Tappan, N.J.: Spire Books, 1959), p. 92.

# 4

# X-Rated Marriages

The home is basically a sacred institution. The perfect
marriage is a uniting of three persons—a man and a
woman and God. That is what makes marriage holy.
Faith in Christ is the most important of all principles in
the building of a happy marriage and a successful home.

—Billy Graham[1]

Not all marriages are made in heaven. When
two unbelievers marry, or when a Christian
and unbeliever marry, they set themselves up
for a lot of heartache. They soon find themselves at
odds. God can bless a marriage of His own people,
but unbelievers take their marriage out of God's hands.
Then it's by no means heavenly. In fact, it can be a hell
on earth.

I call this kind of marriage an "X-rated marriage,"
because it has God's clear stamp of disapproval.

Movie theaters advertise X-rated films with all sorts
of lurid "come-ons" that are supposed to arouse your
interest. They tell you from the very start that the films

are unfit for family viewing. They put an "X" on the ad to warn you that the film has carnal sex, perverted sex, or extreme violence. Yet people attend these films anyway, filling their minds with corruption. In the same way, God warns us against marrying unbelievers; He puts His "X" rating on such a union. He warns us that such marriages always bring trouble. Yet many people plunge ahead and reap the consequences.

Notice what Abraham said to his chief servant Eliezar about marriage: *"Swear by the Lord, the God of heaven, and the God of the earth, that thou shalt not take a wife unto my son of the daughters of the Canaanites, among whom I dwell"* (Gen. 24:3). Abraham did not want his son to marry a woman who came from a pagan and immoral family. He knew that the Canaanites had loose morals. They were steeped in heathen myths and idolatry; they were ungodly to the very core. So he made Eliezar promise before God that he would not let Isaac marry a woman of Canaanite origin.

I think parents are often too careless about the kind of friends they let their children socialize with. This may sound old-fashioned, but I'll say it anyway: We need to be more careful that our sons and daughters have good Christian friends. Because Christian parents have had a "do-your-own-thing" attitude toward their children in recent years, we have seen hundreds of young people lured into ungodly marriages. Careless Christian parents have *"sown the wind, and they shall reap the whirlwind"* (Hos. 8:7).

## The Sorrow of Ungodly Marriage

Ungodliness always brings sorrow. We see that illustrated throughout the world. Until India turns to God, for example, no one will be able to end its poverty and starvation. Until Americans repent and accept the Lord, they will struggle with inflation, crime, and spiritual bankruptcy. The same is true in any individual's life. Ungodliness brings sorrow.

Marriage simply redoubles the sorrow of ungodliness. It solves no problems for an ungodly person; in fact, it gives him a whole new set of problems! This is why the Old Testament patriarchs took pains to tell their children not to marry a heathen. (See Genesis 28:1.) They knew an ungodly marriage would bring their children nothing but trouble and pain.

God reminded His people of this as they prepared to enter the Promised Land. He warned them of the pagan peoples they would find in Canaan, and He said:

> *17. Neither shalt thou make marriages with them; thy daughter thou shalt not give unto his son, nor his daughter shalt thou take unto thy son. For they will turn away thy son from following me, that they may serve other gods: so will the anger of the LORD be kindled against you, and destroy thee suddenly.* (Deut. 7:3–4)

Again we see God's protectiveness about sex. He would not allow His chosen people to marry just anyone, because ungodly marriages make ungodly people. Such marriages are designated "X-rated" because they will corrupt both marriage partners. God gave Israel the same warning through Joshua:

> *18. If ye do in any wise go back, and cleave unto the remnant of these nations, even these that remain among you, and shall make marriages*

*with them, and go in unto them, and they to you: know for a certainty that the LORD your God will no more drive out any of these nations from before you; but they shall be snares and traps unto you.* (Josh. 23:12–13)

You see, this is not only a family problem—it is a national problem. Ungodly marriages undermine the entire nation. They unravel the moral fabric of the society. They warp the values that a decent home should uphold. Why? Because they are not anchored to the rock of God's truth.

If you've never been involved in such a marriage, you may think this restriction is too harsh. You may have an optimistic attitude toward your ungodly mate, saying, "I'll be able to change him (or her) for the better." But sad to say, it usually works the other way around. The ungodly mate will discourage and corrupt the godly one. In fact, the ungodly mate will get his (or her) partner into problems that otherwise would never occur.

Make no mistake: When you marry outside God's family, you step outside His protection. You expose yourself to problems you never would have had otherwise. God says:

*19. Do not be unequally yoked together with unbelievers. For what fellowship has righteousness with lawlessness? And what communion has light with darkness?* (2 Cor. 6:14 NKJV)

Marriage is not the sort of thing you should launch on a whim or impulse. When you marry, you must think not only of yourself but of your children and grandchildren; all of them will be exposed to your marriage. All of them will be affected by the mate you choose. God says that when a believer and an unbeliever marry, it's like a donkey and a camel trying to pull a plow together, they just don't match. One is too tall and the other too short; one takes long strides and the other takes short strides. They don't share the burden equally. They are "unequally yoked."

## Ungodly Marriage in the Bible

In Genesis 6:1–6, we read that the *"sons of God"* married the *"daughters of men"* in outright defiance of God. Bible scholars have long speculated about who the *"sons of God"* were; some say they were a particular tribe of Adam's descendants, others that they were some sort of superhuman, spiritual beings. No matter how you interpret that phrase, it's clear that they were "unequally yoked" with their wives. Godly men married carnal women. The result? God sent the great Flood to destroy that wicked generation, saving only Noah and his family.

Can you imagine that? Ungodly marriages—X-rated marriages—caused the greatest catastrophe the world has ever known.

Samson, one of the judges of Israel, decided to marry a heathen woman from among the Philistines. You'll recall how he came back from Timnath and told his parents, *"Get her for me"* (Judg. 14:2).

Samson's parents were God-fearing people; they knew that marriage was not to be taken lightly. So his father asked, *"Is there never a woman among the daughters of thy brethren, or among all my people, that thou goest to take a wife of the uncircumcised Philistines?"* (v. 3).

But Samson said, *"Get her for me; for she pleaseth me well"* (v. 3). This kind of attitude is widespread today. Young men and women care nothing about the spiritual background of their friends. When they get engaged to marry, they seldom think about what kind of family they're getting into. They only say, "She turns me on," or, "I really like the way he kisses." That seems to be their only standard for choosing a mate. But Samson's X-rated marriage caused him to lose his eyes, to lose his dignity, and even to lose his life with his wife's heathen friends.

What a tragic thing it is to get involved in an ungodly marriage! When you marry the wrong person in open defiance of God, you have no idea what the future holds for you.

It's no use to say, "That's all right. I know what I'm doing." Even King Solomon, one of the wisest men who ever lived, made a foolish mistake when he married heathen women. His X-rated marriages finally destroyed his kingdom.

> *King Solomon loved many strange women, together with the daughter of Pharaoh, women of the Moabites, Ammonites, Edomites, Zidonians, and Hittites; of the nations concerning which the LORD said unto the children of Israel, Ye shall not go in to them, neither shall they come in unto you: for surely they will turn away your heart after their gods: Solomon clave unto these in love.* (1 Kings 11:1–2)

His heathen wives persuaded him to set up altars to their gods, and they gradually got him to worship their gods. In the end, Scripture says, *"his heart was not perfect with the LORD his God, as was the heart of David his father"* (I Kings 11:4). What a sad commentary! Solomon was wise in statecraft and politics, but he acted foolishly in the realm of sex. He was "unequally yoked."

## Practical Answers

This is not to say that a Christian who winds up in an ungodly marriage just has to "tough it out." God admonishes a Christian in such a situation to set a good example for his or her mate. Notice His word to wives especially:

> *20. Wives, likewise, be submissive to your own husbands, that even if some do not obey the word, they, without a word, may be won by the conduct of their wives.* (1 Pet. 3:1 NKJV)

Dorothy C. Haskin spent several years trying to win her husband to the Lord. Both of them were unbelievers when they married, and she was converted just one year later. At first she tried to make him attend church services with her. "The result was that he decided I was a 'religious fanatic,' and he was not interested in my faith," she says.[2] But she kept on trying. She subscribed to some good Christian magazines, which he picked up and casually leafed through. She occasionally tuned in Christian radio programs for their leisure-time listening. She invited him to church for some special occasions. But even though she saw a breakthrough now and then, it wasn't easy.

> I liked to attend all the services but I realized that he would not. I gave up some so he would attend the others. Because he had to get up early Monday morning and liked to take his mother for a long drive after dinner on Sunday, I decided that

Sunday school was easiest for him. So we went to Sunday school. Later, he decided he preferred the eleven o'clock Sunday service.

My husband received Christ as Savior in his forties and was baptized. Nothing takes more tact and patience than winning a non-Christian husband to the Lord.[3]

I'm sure that many other people caught in X-rated marriages would say the same thing. It's a long, tough battle to win an unbelieving mate to the Lord. But if you're patient, you may see results. *"Let us not grow weary while doing good, for in due season we shall reap if we do not lose heart"* (Gal. 6:9 NKJV).

If you are married to an unbeliever, I want you to know that God still loves you and cares for you. He can forgive your mistake. An X-rated marriage can bring you deep sorrow, sadness, and even damnation of the soul. You can get so far from God that it seems there's no way back. But God is always ready to welcome you back when you realize your mistake.

If you are contemplating marriage, be sure that you are getting married in three ways—in body, soul, and spirit. If you are married in all three ways, you are destined to have a happy marriage and a harmonious home.

# Notes

1. Joan Winmill Brown, ed., *Day-by-Day with Billy Graham* (Minneapolis: World Wide Publications, 1976), May 27.

2. Dorothy C. Haskin, *God in My Home* (Anderson, Ind.: Portal Books, 1973), p. 12.

3 Ibid., p. 16.

# 5

# Sex and Divorce

A crisis is a fork in the road—the couple turns either
toward growth or toward greater alienation.

—Howard J. Clinebell, Jr.[1]

Hardly any family in America has not been
affected by divorce. It is a problem that grips
our society like an octopus, strangling the very
life out of our families. Even Christian marriages are
dissolving in divorce. In fact, statistics show that one
out of every three new marriages will end in divorce.
The problem has become a national menace.

Sex is very closely related to the divorce problem.
Some divorces result from sexual problems *per se;* in
others, sexual problems play a major role. I believe that
a husband and wife who completely share one another
in the sexual relationship are not likely to ask for
a divorce. Their differences will be minimized, and
any conflicts that do crop up can be discussed openly
and maturely. A healthy sexual relationship helps to
preserve a healthy marriage. By the same token, an

unhealthy sexual relationship does nothing to stop the disintegration of a marriage—and may speed it up.

Divorce is an admission of failure. It means that a husband and wife have failed to make the adjustments of marriage. (And believe me, any marriage calls for adjustments!) Divorce means that a man and woman have chosen to go their separate ways instead of facing their problems head-on and trying to solve them.

# Immaturity

More often than not, divorce is a couple's surrender flag in the battle for maturity. It's true! Many married couples are immature from the start. They have no idea of the responsibilities marriage will entail; and when the responsibilities are dumped in their laps, they don't know what to do. Lester David tells of such a marriage:

> It was a beautiful wedding. True, the bride was only sixteen and the groom just nineteen, but they looked grown-up as they stood there, she so radiant, he so tall and protecting. No one could foretell that less than a year later this fine young man would say to this lovely girl, "I wish you were dead, because then I'd be free." Or that, later the same day, she would slash her wrists.[2]

How could such a couple stand a chance? They were scarcely adults in the physical sense, and certainly not in the spiritual, emotional, or intellectual sense. So they could not be sexually mature. They could not handle the stresses of living together day after day. They "got on each other's nerves," so their marriage became a curse instead of a blessing. Divorce was their way of withdrawing from the battlefield and nursing their wounds after her attempted suicide.

## Casual Attitude

To some extent, divorce is caused by our society's casual attitude toward marriage. Many people think that marriage is simply a "convenient arrangement" that they can begin or terminate as they wish, much like signing a lease on an apartment. When you tire of the scenery, you simply pack your bags and leave. This kind of attitude shows a basic disregard for the spiritual side of marriage. Just after World War II, when the divorce rate in America was growing at an alarming rate, the sociologist Henry A. Bowman made this comment:

> Marriages contracted with a civil ceremony are more likely to end in divorce than those contracted with a religious ceremony. This does not mean that an irreligious couple could increase the probability of their marital success by having a minister marry them. The type of ceremony is significant only to the degree to which it reflects the attitudes of the parties to the union.[3]

Dr. Bowman closed his remarks with this pointed note:

> Those [marriages] more deeply affected by the decline of religious authority are less likely to succeed, or, at any rate, are more likely to divorce.[4]

Remember this is a sociologist speaking, not a minister. He says that couples who have little regard for their spiritual life are more likely to fail in marriage. They are more likely to break up. They lack a vital ingredient of the cement that should hold a marriage together, because they are married in only two ways—in body and soul, but not in spirit.

Remember that divorce is a breakdown of the moral and spiritual fibers that bind a couple to one another. If they cut the spiritual strands that God used to wed them as husband and wife, they will find little else in common. They will become disenchanted and dissatisfied with one another.

## Misguided Ideals

Many couples wind up in divorce court because they had a misguided notion of marriage to begin with. A romanticized picture of what marriage would be like made them unable to cope with the harsh reality that they found the morning after their wedding day. Dr. Clyde M. Narramore tells of a young lady who brought a folder full of poetry to the editorial office of a large publishing house, hoping to have her work accepted for a leading magazine. When she finally was ushered into the editor's office, she gaily informed him that she had some love poems for his publication.

"Well, what is love? Tell me," the editor said.

The girl's eyes got misty and she heaved a happy sigh. "Love is filling one's soul with the beauties of the night," she murmured, "by the shimmering moonbeams on the lily pond when the fragrant lilies are in bloom, and..."

"Stop, stop, stop!" the editor exclaimed. "You are all wrong. I'll tell you what love is: It's getting up cheerfully out of a warm bed in the middle of the night to clean up after a sick child. That's real love."[5]

# Sex and Divorce

Thousands of young couples march down the wedding aisle with the sort of visions this girl described, only to find a couple of years later that the editor's picture of love was more realistic. It's an unpleasant surprise. And some marriages don't survive the shock.

## Selfishness

Selfishness is another common cause of divorce. One or both partners begin to say, "I don't get the attention I'm supposed to get from this marriage," or "Why doesn't he (or she) give me the love I'm supposed to get?" Bickering starts. Husband and wife make subtle digs at each other. They use "hostile humor" to get revenge because they think they have been shortchanged. Just like two nations beginning a war, the minor skirmishes get worse; the mates attack each other more and more caustically. Soon the hatred boils over into divorce.

This is a symptom of the decadent society in America today. Our nation is becoming more unstable, which in turn causes individuals to become more unstable. Marriage partners begin growling and fussing at one another for any little excuse, and they are more prone to run to the divorce court for a final solution. But the courts do not solve the problem—they simply bring it to a conclusion. Lawyers specializing in divorce cases are becoming quite wealthy, and they don't do it by counseling their clients away from divorce! Judges render decisions that have no basis in the Bible or even in common human decency; they just follow precedent. They keep on repeating the mistakes of other judges before them. A judge in Ft. Lauderdale once told me, "You must realize, Mr. Sumrall, that there are times when the court is God."

"Sir, the court can never replace God," I replied.

You had better believe it! God is sovereign above all human beings, above all courts, above all cultures. Governments may rise and fall, but God remains the same. Our first loyalty is not to the law books of our land but to the Law Book of our God. When we obey His law, we will have no problem meeting the loose requirements of man's law.

# God's Word on Divorce

Many marriage counselors—even some ministers— would say that divorce is the best solution for a serious marriage problem. But is that the advice God would give? What does He have to say about divorce? Jesus told the Pharisees:

> 21. *Moses, because of the hardness of your hearts, permitted you to divorce your wives, but from the beginning it was not so. And I say to you, whoever divorces his wife, except for sexual immorality, and marries another, commits adultery; and whoever marries her who is divorced commits adultery.*
> (*Matt. 19:8–9* NKJV)[6]

A person could interpret this passage to suit his own preconceived ideas about divorce, but I think it speaks for itself Jesus is saying exactly what He means: *Divorce is wrong.*

Notice that He said, *"From the beginning it was not so."* God ordained marriage from the very beginning, but not divorce. Only later, when man and woman corrupted marriage with adultery and all sorts of perversion did God find it necessary to permit divorce. It was better to make a formal separation between a husband and wife than to let them display their corrupt relationship to the whole community. Read closely the specific law that God gave for divorce:

*22. When a man hath taken a wife, and married her, and it come to pass that she find no favour in his eyes, because he hath found some uncleanness in her: then let him write her a bill of divorcement, and give it in her hand, and send her out of his house. And when she is departed out of his house, she may go and be another man's wife.* (Deut. 24:1–2)[7]

God said that if a man found *"some uncleanness"* in his wife—if she were an adulteress—he did not have to live with her. He could give her a *"bill of divorcement"* and make a formal end to their marriage. That was the only reason for which God allowed divorce.

Yet the people of Israel took advantage of this statute. They began to grant divorces over very trivial things. The rulers took liberty with the phrase, *"she find no favor in his eyes,"* and interpreted it to mean any sort of dislike or displeasure the husband had with his wife. In fact, many Jewish women lived in terror of their husbands, always fearing that they would be divorced in a fit of anger, being left to fend for themselves. So God spoke through the prophet Malachi to clarify this law:

*23. The LORD hath been witness between thee and the wife of thy youth, against whom thou hast dealt treacherously: yet is she thy companion,*

*and the wife of thy covenant. And did not he
make one?...And wherefore one? That he might
seek a godly seed. Therefore take heed to your
spirit, and let none deal treacherously against
the wife of his youth. For the LORD, the God of
Israel, saith that he hateth putting away: for
one covereth violence with his garment, saith the
LORD of hosts: therefore take heed to your spirit,
that ye deal not treacherously.* (Mal. 2:14–16)

God hates divorce! He is not pleased when a husband and wife sever themselves from one another.
Frankly, I would do everything I could to avoid doing
something that God hates; I would try to find some
other way to rectify the situation. Divorce is the great
"cover-up" of marital sins—yet God sees right through
the cover! He knows what really happened, and He
hates it.

God gave the Israelites strict rules to prevent any
slaphappy use of divorce. For example, a bride's family
was supposed to keep the bedding from a couple's wedding night. Then if the man falsely accused her of fornication, they could show the bloodstained evidence of
her virginity:

*24. If any man take a wife, and go in unto
her, and hate her, and give occasions of speech
against her, and bring up an evil name upon her,
and say, I took this woman, and when I came
to her, I found her not a maid: then shall the
father of the damsel, and her mother, take and
bring forth the tokens of the damsel's virginity
unto the elders of the city in the gate: and the*

*damsel's father shall say unto the elders, I gave my daughter unto this man to wife, and he hateth her; and, lo, he hath given occasions of speech against her,...and yet these are the tokens of my daughter's virginity. And they shall spread the cloth before the elders of the city. And the elders of that city shall take that man and chastise him; and they shall amerce him in an hundred shekels of silver, and give them unto the father of the damsel, because he hath brought up an evil name upon a virgin of Israel: and she shall be his wife; he may not put her away all his days.*

*(Deut. 22:13–19)*

Some people get married and at first things seem to go well; but eventually they start blaming and accusing one another. They try to say their spouse has ruined the marriage by having sex with someone else. But God will expose the truth, either now or later.

I did say He was protective about sex, didn't I?

God also laid down strict rules to govern remarriage after divorce. You will recall, for example, that the passage from Deuteronomy 24 allowed a divorced woman to remarry. But take a careful look at what God then says:

*25. And if the latter husband hate her, and write her a bill of divorcement, and giveth it in her hand, and sendeth her out of his house...her former husband, which sent her away, may not take her again to be his wife, after that she is defiled; for that is abomination before the LORD.*

*(Deut. 24:3–4)*

You see, God does not approve of any Hollywood-style marriages. Capriciously marrying one person after another is an "abomination" in His sight. So far as He is concerned, a divorced woman who has remarried is now "defiled" unto her former husband, and her first husband would corrupt himself by marrying her again.

Even when God permitted divorce, He regulated it to make sure that no one used divorce as an excuse for promiscuity.

## Better Solutions

If you are having problems with your marriage, consider your alternatives besides divorce. By all means, seek the advice of a capable Christian counselor. Your pastor may be able to do this; if not, he should refer you to someone who can. But the first step in dealing with your problem is being able to talk about it, and a good counselor can help you do that.

If you have children, your counselor might even recommend family counseling; in other words, he may want to bring the whole family together in his office to talk about your problem. You may not want to do that in order to protect your children from the hurts of your marriage. But whether you like it or not, the children are a part of the hurting, and it's best to let them be a part of the healing. The noted family counselor Virginia Satir says:

> Once the therapist convinces the husband that he is essential to the therapy process, and that no one else can speak for him or take his place in therapy *or* in family life, he readily enters in. The wife (in her role as mother) may initiate family

therapy, but once therapy is underway, the husband becomes as involved as she does. Family therapy seems to make sense to the whole family. Husband and wife say: "Now, at last, we are together and can get to the bottom of this."[8]

Both of you need to face your problem and admit that it is a problem. Your family needs to face it. In fact, you may find that your family grows stronger as you sit down together and talk through your marital trouble.

Have a forgiving spirit toward one another. Don't be afraid to reconsider what you've done and say, "You know, I was wrong. I am sorry." This kind of spirit would eliminate the vast majority of all divorces. But an obstinate, unforgiving spirit continues to drag old problems up out of the cellar and hurl them at everyone else. The result is broken hearts and broken homes. Jesus is our example of forgiveness; if we imitate His spirit of love and understanding toward our mates, we will bring harmony back to the most disharmonious situations.

Speaking of forgiveness—notice that adultery can be forgiven, just like any other sin. Some Christians think that God requires divorce for adultery, even if the sinful mate repents of what he or she has done. But look back at what He said. He doesn't require divorce for adultery; He allows it. He then says that He hates divorce, period.

It is far better to forgive than to punish a person forever. If you hold a grudge against your mate, you inject poison into your own veins. You make yourself a bitter person. You cause yourself as much suffering as your mate—often more. But if you extend the hand of love to your mate, you will find your love returned. You will grow stronger and more mature as a Christian. Dr. G. Curtis Jones tells of such a case:

> I once served a church where the chief custodian had been on the staff for fifty years. During this time he had serious domestic troubles. His wife left him. Years passed. Eventually she asked to return. This splendid Christian took her back, saying, "She is my wife and the mother of my son." Such forgiveness is reminiscent of Hosea, who received again his wife after her unfaithfulness. Little wonder that the congregation served by this man erected a plaque to his memory.[9]

If your mate commits adultery, I urge you to read the book of Hosea and learn what forgiveness really means. Think about the love Hosea had for his wife, who kept sliding back into promiscuity. The Law allowed him to divorce her, and he certainly would have felt justified in doing so. But his love won out. He forgave her and brought her back home. Together they reestablished their family.

I want your home to be beautiful. I want Jesus to bless your marriage. If you are having a marital problem, go to the Bible together and see what God says about it. Then pray together and let the Spirit of the Lord fill you anew. Let His forgiveness flow into your hearts. Then talk with each other about your problem. Take the first step to heal the wounds in your relationship by saying, "I'm sorry, Honey. I've been wrong."

"But, Dr. Sumrall," you say, "I haven't been wrong!"

Friend, it takes two people to disagree. It takes two to have discord. It takes two to break up a marriage. So no matter whether you were "right" or "wrong" about the issue that started your trouble, you were wrong to let it develop into trouble. Admit that. Ask for your mate's forgiveness. Then God can begin bringing you back together.

# Notes

1. Howard J. Clinebell, Jr., *Growth Counseling for Marriage Enrichment* (Philadelphia: Fortress Press, 1975), p. 65.

2. Lester David, "Matrimony Is Not for Children," *How to Live with Life* (Pleasantville, N.Y.: Reader's Digest Association, 1965), p. 44.

3. Henry A. Bowman, *Marriage for Moderns* (New York: McGraw-Hill, 1954), p. 502.

4. Ibid., p. 502.

5. Clyde M. Narramore, *This Way to Happiness* (Grand Rapids, Mich.: Zondervan, 1969), p. 22.

6. Apparently the last portion of this text refers to a woman who was divorced for reasons other than adultery. That is to say, if a man marries a woman divorced for an illegitimate reason, he is committing adultery.

7. The last phrase of this passage does not condone adultery, because God does not condone it. The intent, I assume, is to allow a divorced adulteress who has *repented* to remarry.

8. Virginia Satir, *Conjoint Family Therapy*, rev. ed. (Palo Alto, Calif.: Science and Behavior Books, Inc., 1967), p. 5.

9. G. Curtis Jones, *A Man and His Religion* (St. Louis: Bethany, 1967), p. 65.

# 6

# Twenty Laws against Incest

To an age which condones increasingly the exploitation
of human beings in the game of sex, [God's Word] speaks
of the divine order among men, requiring recognition of
the sanctity of marriage. People are not simply bodies to
be played with.

—Jack Ford[1]

The *Phil Donahue Show* recently featured a young
woman whose stepfather had sexual relations
with her many times while she was a teenager.
This bond of incest nearly destroyed her, emotionally
and spiritually. Her stepfather repented of what he had
done, and through the help of experienced counselors
the young woman was able to regain her sense of dignity and self-respect.

"What I did was a terrible thing," the stepfather
said. "But I hope that our telling about it will help some
other family avoid this problem."

Incest is one of the "secret sins" that people seldom discuss. It is a vile sin. It destroys the family as a unit and individuals within that family. But worst of all, it offends God, who created sex for marriage.

God ordained that a man and woman who have the same parents or who are closely related by blood should not cohabit. They should not share sexual intimacy. They should not produce offspring. A person might think that God would avoid such a delicate topic, but the Bible is loaded with God's pronouncements on incest. In fact, the Bible repeats His law against incest at least twenty times, and in two different books of the Old Testament. Read God's commandment against incest and the rationale behind it:

*26. None of you shall approach to any that is near of kin to him, to uncover their nakedness: I am the LORD.* (Lev. 18:6)

Scripture uses the phrase *"to uncover their nakedness"* as a tactful way of referring to sexual intercourse. God specifically says that a person should not have intercourse with someone who is *"near of kin."* Why? Because *"I am the LORD"*—in other words, it's so, simply because He has the authority to say so. Now notice the specific cases of incest that God forbids:

*27. The nakedness of thy father, or the nakedness of thy mother, shalt thou not uncover: she is thy mother; thou shalt not uncover her nakedness. The nakedness of thy father's wife shalt thou not uncover: it is thy father's nakedness.*
(Lev. 18:7–8)

# Twenty Laws against Incest

To put it plainly, God says that a girl should not have sexual relations with her father and a boy should not have sexual relations with his mother.

"But, Brother Sumrall," someone is likely to say, "That just doesn't happen anymore!"

As a pastor, I can tell you that it happens all the time. I constantly have people coming into my office who are caught up in incest. For example, I've counseled with a young man who ran away from home because his mother insisted on having intercourse with him. The first time he ever had sexual relations with a woman was when she seduced him into her bed, and she insisted that she "teach" him the way to have sexual pleasure. Anytime she wished, she forced him into bed with her by threatening to tell his father. Don't say that God is just talking into the wind when He talks about incest; He is talking to the homes of America. He forbids anyone to defile the marriage of mother and father.

*28. The nakedness of thy sister, the daughter of thy father, or daughter of thy mother, whether she be born at home, or born abroad, even their nakedness thou shalt not uncover.    (Lev. 18:9)*

*29. The nakedness of thy son's daughter, or of thy daughter's daughter, even their nakedness thou shalt not uncover: for theirs is thine own nakedness.    (Lev. 18:10)*

*30. The nakedness of thy father's wife's daughter, begotten of thy father, she is thy sister, thou shalt not uncover her nakedness.    (Lev. 18:11)*

*31. Thou shalt not uncover the nakedness of thy father's sister: she is thy father's near kinswoman. Thou shalt not uncover the nakedness of thy mother's sister; for she is thy mother's near kinswoman. Thou shalt not uncover the nakedness of thy father's brother, thou shalt not approach to his wife: she is thine aunt.      (Lev. 18:12–14)*

*32. Thou shalt not uncover the nakedness of thy daughter in law: she is thy son's wife; thou shalt not uncover her nakedness.            (Lev. 18:15)*

*33. Thou shalt not uncover the nakedness of thy brother's wife: it is thy brother's nakedness.*
*(Lev. 18:16)*

*34. Thou shalt not uncover the nakedness of a woman and her daughter, neither shalt thou take her son's daughter, or her daughter's daughter, to uncover her nakedness; for they are her near kinswomen: it is wickedness. Neither shalt thou take a wife to her sister, to vex her, to uncover her nakedness, beside the other in her life time.*
*(Lev. 18:17–18)*

This last law concerns incest in second marriages—incest with stepchildren or other relatives of a second wife. This is perhaps the most common form of incest in America today. With the great number of divorces and remarriages now occurring, men and women are being thrown into intimate contact with new families, and they seem to feel less guilt about having illicit sex with members of these families.

# Twenty Laws against Incest

Recently a woman came to my office for counseling about such a problem. She was married and had two fine children, but she was haunted by the guilt of an incestuous relationship she had had with her stepfather.

When her natural father died, her mother remarried. One day the stepfather sent her mother out to do some shopping, and used the occasion to lure the girl into bed. She was only thirteen at the time. For the next five years, the stepfather kept on arranging these afternoon rendezvous. He said that if she told her mother, he would put the girl out of their house and she would "starve to death." She escaped from that situation only when she got married. But even now the memory of that affair makes her seethe with anger.

You know, sin is a terrible thing! Its effects linger on for years. It leaves scars that take a long time to heal.

*35. And the man that lieth with his father's wife hath uncovered his father's nakedness: both of them shall surely be put to death; their blood shall be upon them.* (Lev. 20:11)

*36. And if a man lie with his daughter in law, both of them shall surely be put to death: they have wrought confusion; their blood shall be upon them.* (Lev. 20:12)

*37. And if a man take a wife and her mother, it is wickedness: they shall be burnt with fire, both he and they; that there be no wickedness among you.* (Lev. 20:14)

*38. And if a man shall take his sister, his father's daughter, or his mother's daughter, and see her*

81

*nakedness, and she see his nakedness; it is a*
*wicked thing; and they shall be cut off in the*
*sight of their people: he hath uncovered his sister's*
*nakedness; he shall bear his iniquity.*

*(Lev. 20:17)*

These laws spell out the penalties for incest. While the laws of chapter 18 simply say that God forbids incest, chapter 20 shows us the consequences of breaking His Word. Obviously, incest was a serious matter. It was punishable in Old Testament times by death—even the torturous death of being burned alive.

But some of God's laws suggest a spiritual penalty for this kind of perversion. We caught a glimpse of that in verse 17, when God said that a man who commits incest with his sister will *"bear his iniquity."* Read on and it becomes clearer that incest brings a spiritual as well as a physical punishment:

*39. And thou shalt not uncover the nakedness of*
*thy mother's sister, nor of thy father's sister: for*
*he uncovereth his near kin: they shall bear their*
*iniquity. And if a man shall lie with his uncle's*
*wife, he hath uncovered his uncle's nakedness:*
*they shall bear their sin; they shall die childless.*

*(Lev. 20:19–20)*

*40. And if a man shall take his brother's wife,*
*it is an unclean thing: he hath uncovered his*
*brother's nakedness; they shall be childless.*

*(Lev. 20:21)*

Not only would the community punish people guilty of incest, but God would punish them by leaving them childless. Incest was such an abomination in His sight that He refused to grant even the normal biological results of intercourse. He would not countenance bringing children into the world under those circumstances.

Unfortunately, that is not true today. Children sometimes are born to incestuous couples. I don't know why God allows this now; perhaps it is because we live in a new era of grace, when everyone has the opportunity to know His law. Perhaps He expects us to be more responsible than the children of Israel were, so He lets us live with the results of our sin. Whatever the reason, I think you would agree that incest brings great spiritual harm as well as emotional harm to the people who are involved.

The book of Deuteronomy is a review and summation of the law that God gave His people at Mount Sinai. This is how the book got its present name, "Deuteronomy" (Greek, "second law"). As we read God's laws against incest in Deuteronomy, we find that the laws of Leviticus have been expanded and clarified at some points:

*41. A man shall not take his father's wife, nor discover his father's skirt.* (Deut. 22:30)

*42. Cursed be he that setteth light by his father or his mother. And all the people shall say, Amen.* (Deut. 27:16)

*43. Cursed be he that lieth with his father's wife; because he uncovereth his father's skirt. And all the people shall say, Amen.* (Deut. 27:20)

*44. Cursed be he that lieth with his sister, the daughter of his father, or the daughter of his*

*mother. And all the people shall say, Amen.*
*(Deut. 27:22)*

*45. Cursed be he that lieth with his mother in*
*law. And all the people shall say, Amen.*
*(Deut. 27:23)*

The first of these laws simply declares that incest is wrong—emphasizing once again that it is wrong just because God says so. But the next four laws put incest in a community perspective. Each one says that the people of Israel were to condemn incest as being *"cursed"*; they were supposed to add their *"amen"* to the priest's pronouncement of the curse. They were responsible for enforcing God's law. The same is true today; God expects us to enforce His laws of sexual morality and condemn any uncleanness that creeps into our society. This is one reason why I felt such a burden to write this book!

## Bible Case Histories

The Bible gives us some case histories of incest, real-life examples of what happened when people ignored God's law. We won't dwell on these long. But I think we should examine how God's laws on incest can protect us from some very foolish and destructive mistakes.

Genesis 35 records a case of incest among the twelve sons of Jacob. Notice what happened:

*And it came to pass, when Israel [Jacob] dwelt in that*
*land, that Reuben went and lay with Bilhah his father's*
*concubine: and Israel heard it.* (Gen. 35:22)

# Twenty Laws against Incest

We read nothing more about this incident until several years later, as Jacob lay on his deathbed. He gathered his twelve sons around him and began to give them his final blessing, Reuben being the first:

*Reuben, thou art my firstborn, my might, and the beginning of my strength, the excellency of dignity, and the excellency of power: unstable as water, thou shalt not excel; because thou wentest up to thy father's bed; then defiledst thou it: he went up to my couch.*

(Gen. 49:3–4)

Can you imagine the shame Reuben must have felt? He was the firstborn son, the legal heir of Jacob's finest possessions; yet Jacob could not bless him because of his incest. Reuben's father revealed his sin in front of his brothers. He said, *"He went up to my couch."* Things probably got so quiet you could hear a pin drop! The brothers were astonished to hear about the crime, and Reuben himself was shamed into silence.

But this wasn't the end of it. Generations later, a Jewish chronicler put this sad note in the record:

*Now the sons of Reuben the firstborn of Israel, (for he was the firstborn; but, forasmuch as he defiled his father's bed, his birthright was given unto the sons of Joseph the son of Israel: and the genealogy is not to be reckoned after the birthright.)* (1 Chron. 5:1)

Reuben lost his birthright. He lost his rightful inheritance because he had an affair with his father's concubine. So the chronicler begged our indulgence to list Reuben's descendants. "After all," he says, "I have to do it because the genealogy is reckoned according to the firstborn, not according to the birthright." Reuben

85

put a blight on his family—a blight on history itself—by indulging himself in an impulsive fling with his father's mate.

Another case of incest is recorded in 2 Samuel 16. This occurred in the family of David, the greatest king of Israel:

> *Then said Absalom to Ahithophel, Give counsel among you what we shall do. And Ahithophel said unto Absalom, Go in unto thy father's concubines, which he hath left to keep the house; and all Israel shall hear that thou art abhorred of thy father: then shall the hands of all that are with thee be strong. So they spread Absalom a tent upon the top of the house; and Absalom went in unto his father's concubines in the sight of all Israel.*
> (2 Sam. 16:20–22)

Absalom wanted to start a rebellion against his father, so he asked the king's counselor (who was plotting with him) how to get the people stirred up. "That's simple," the counselor said, "just pitch a tent on top of your father's house, where everyone can see you, and have sex with all of his mistresses!"

So Absalom took the advice. He committed incest with his father's women. And the nation erupted into a vicious civil war that ended only with Absalom's death. Actually, this was a fulfillment of prophecy. When King David had conspired to get the wife of Uriah the Hittite, the prophet Nathan confronted him with these words:

> *Thus saith the LORD, Behold, I will raise up evil against thee out of thine own house, and I will take thy wives before thine eyes, and give them unto thy neighbour, and he shall lie with thy wives in the sight of this sun.*
> (2 Sam. 12: 11)

# Twenty Laws against Incest

When sin comes back to you, it comes back with a vengeance. No one learned this lesson more painfully than David.

At least one case of incest is recorded in the New Testament. In fact, Paul devoted an entire chapter of his first letter to the Corinthians to this problem. He wrote,

> *It is actually reported that there is sexual immorality among you, and such sexual immorality as is not even named among the Gentiles; that a man has his father's wife!...Deliver such a one to Satan for the destruction of the flesh, that his spirit may be saved in the day of the Lord Jesus.* (1 Cor. 5:1, 5 NKJV)

The man committing incest was a Christian. We know this because Paul mentions him again in 2 Corinthians 2 and calls him a "brother." Yet the man was living in sin with his father's wife, and the church did nothing to correct it. So Paul rebuked them. He said, *"Do you not know that a little leaven leavens the whole lump?"* (1 Cor. 5:6 NKJV). In other words, if they let one man live in incest, they would soon have other Christians living in adultery or homosexuality or Christian girls walking the streets as prostitutes. They had to get rid of the sin. So Paul told them to expel the man from their fellowship. It was better to make him live outside the church without all the physical benefits that the first-century church provided, and hope that he would realize his sin and repent.

In fact, that's what happened. The church put him out. And apparently the man repented, for in Paul's next letter he said,

> *This punishment which was inflicted by the majority is sufficient for such a man, so that, on the contrary, you*

*ought rather to forgive and comfort him, lest perhaps such a one be swallowed up with too much sorrow.*

(2 Cor. 2:6-7 NKJV)

God's forgiveness is that complete: He can forgive any sexual sin, even incest, if a person repents of it. God says that we are not to pervert the purpose of sex by having intercourse with our parents, our children, or other next of kin. Sex is not just another family entertainment. It is a holy and wholesome thing that ought to be respected and used reverently.

# Notes

1. Jack Ford, "The Book of Deuteronomy," *Beacon Bible Commentary*, vol. 1, ed. A. F. Harper (Kansas City: Beacon Hill, 1969), p. 578.

# 7

# Sexual Perversion
# Bears a Curse

Some people are building chicken coops when they
ought to be erecting mansions. Remember you will have
to live in what you build. You can build a chicken coop
and be cooped up all your life, or you can build a
mansion and enjoy the freedom of its comforts.

—Carl C. Williams[1]

No person has ever been born a homosexual.
Yet thousands of people in our country believe
they are different by design. They believe there
is some natural alteration in their body chemistry that
draws them to persons of the same sex, and they say
they ought to have a free and open homosexual relationship. But God's Word says they are wrong. A homosexual becomes so through lust, which leads to experimentation, or through the pressure of homosexual
or bisexual friends or relatives. It is not what God
intended.

Before the slogans of "gay rights" became so popular, homosexual acts were called "sodomy." That term comes from the city of Sodom, which the Bible describes as one of the most wicked cities on the face of the earth. Genesis 19 tells how God sent two angels to visit Lot in that city. As they sat around their evening meal, the men of Sodom pounded on the door and demanded that Lot send his visitors out so they could have sexual relations with them. Lot begged the men to take his daughters instead. But the mob was intent upon having the men. While they argued about it, the angels struck the crowd blind. Then they warned Lot to gather his family and flee from the city, saying that God had sent them to destroy it because of its great sinfulness.

This account proves that sexual perversion did not begin in the twentieth century; it has been with us ever since the Fall of Adam and Eve. But it is just as foul and damnable today as it was in the days of Sodom.

## God's Word for "Gays"

God has given us a very explicit ruling on homosexuality. Read what His Word says:

*46. Thou shalt not lie with mankind, as with womankind: it is abomination....Defile not ye yourselves in any of these things: for in all these the nations are defiled which I cast out before you: and the land is defiled: therefore I do visit the iniquity thereof upon it, and the land itself vomiteth out her inhabitants.* (Lev. 18:22, 24–25)

God wiped out entire nations because they practiced homosexuality. Did you know that was in the Bible? It's a terrible thing to think about.

# Sexual Perversion Bears a Curse

Amidst all the clamor for "gay rights," we ought to pay careful attention to what God says about homosexuality. God takes this problem seriously, and He deals with it firmly. He classes homosexuality among the most vile sins of humankind.

*47. For even their women exchanged the natural use [of sex] for what is against nature. Likewise also the men, leaving the natural use of the woman, burned in their lust for one another, men with men committing what is shameful, and receiving in themselves the penalty of their error which was due....those who practice such things are deserving of death.* (Rom. 1:26–27,32 NKJV)

Would God say this about homosexuals if some people were *born* this way? I think not. He is trying to protect us from unnatural passions. Homosexuality is just as perverse as prostitution; both warp the purpose God intended for sex. Read what He says:

*48. There shall be no whore of the daughters of Israel, nor a sodomite of the sons of Israel.*
(Deut. 23:17)

God uses strong language to denounce the perversion of sex. As we have seen so many times before, God is very protective of sex. He leaves no room for behavior that is motivated by twisted lust.

I have had enough face-to-face encounters with homosexuals to know what a sad and desperate life they lead. While I was walking through the streets of Jerusalem, for example, I was approached by several young boys offering to have sexual relations with me.

These were very young boys—about ten years old. I can't tell you how much this grieved my heart. But I put my arm around the shoulders of each little boy and said, "Son, I don't know what kind of men you've met before, but I am a godly man, and I want you to know that what you're doing is wrong. It is wrong to offer to do such a thing—it is wicked. You go right home and tell your parents what you've been doing, and ask God to forgive you for this."

This kind of thing has gone on for centuries, and is now common in America. Homosexuality is drawing thousands of men and women into its spell.

> *49. Do you not know that the unrighteous will not inherit the kingdom of God? Do not be deceived. Neither fornicators, nor idolaters, nor adulterers, nor homosexuals, nor sodomites, nor thieves, nor covetous, nor drunkards, nor revilers, nor extortioners will inherit the kingdom of God.*
> *(1 Cor. 6:9–10 NKJV)*

This is the worst thing about homosexuality—the spiritual result. Granted, it degrades the individual and distorts his moral values. Sex becomes a flippant kind of physical recreation that can be enjoyed anytime, anywhere, with anybody. These results are bad enough. But the clincher is what homosexuality does to the soul of a person, leading him or her into gross sin.

The Bible says that homosexuality ranks beside drunkenness, extortion, and idolatry as a despicable form of ungodliness. It declares that a homosexual cannot inherit the kingdom of God, anymore than a common thief could. If you think God is being too harsh at this point, remember the basic purposes of sex:

# Sexual Perversion Bears a Curse

*—To bring children into the world.* Homosexuals and lesbians cannot fulfill God's first commandment regarding sex (Gen. 1:28). They cannot *"replenish the earth"* through their perverse cavorting. In fact, if everyone thought homosexuality was the ideal model for a sex life, humanity would die out in one generation.

*—To give pleasure to married partners.* Some homosexuals try to circumvent this by staging "gay marriages"—actually getting married to their sexual partners. But God still says it is sinful for two people of the same sex to "make love" to one another (Lev. 18:22), and the sanction of an attorney or justice of the peace doesn't make it less wrong.

*—To symbolize Christ's relationship with His church* (Eph. 5:23–25). In this respect, homosexuality is an outright blasphemy against God. It suggests, in effect, that Christ has no love for His church or that the church has no need for Christ. Either statement is a lie. A homosexual is perverting the truth of God as well as perverting sex, the gift of God. This sin must be named for what it really is.

Yet even the sin of homosexuality can be forgiven. Leaders of the "gay rights" movement insist that homosexuality is something that a person must live with forever; but God doesn't say that. He says, *"Come now, and let us reason together...though your sins be as scarlet, they shall be as white as snow; though they be red like crimson, they shall be as wool"* (Isa. 1:18). God is ready to forgive any sin, no matter how vile and offensive it is, as soon as we confess our sin to Him. He loves us that much. One of my favorite verses of the Bible says, *"If we confess our sins, he is faithful and just to forgive us our sins, and to cleanse us from all unrighteousness"* (1 John 1:9). It's true! When we confess our sins to the Lord, He will forgive us and wash all the sin out of our lives—even the sin of homosexuality.

Don't be fooled into thinking that homosexuality is something in your genes, something that can't be changed. It is a sin. And thank God, sin can be wiped out when we confess it to Him.

# Prostitution

I have focused a lot of attention on the perversion of homosexuality simply because God's Word is being challenged so boldly on that point these days. But we ought not to overlook other forms of sexual perversion that are just as sinful and devastating. One of these is prostitution.

Prostitution is the selling of one's sexual favors. It is the merchandising of sex—having intercourse with someone for money or some other privilege. There are both female and male prostitutes, and they operate in all levels of society. A federal judge was recently indicted on charges of taking sexual favors from female defendants. A wealthy prostitute in Washington, D.C., named several high-ranking politicians as her customers in a scandal just a few years ago. Many movie stars and corporation executives keep their prostitutes in well-heeled comfort, letting them live in expensive apartments and be chauffeured about town in plush limousines. Prostitution is not just a Skid Row enterprise anymore. One sociologist has made this cold assessment of the problem:

> Prostitution has perdured [sic] in all civilizations; indeed, few institutions have proven as hardy. The inevitable conditions of social life unfailingly produce the supply to meet the ever-present demand.[2]

## Sexual Perversion Bears a Curse

He goes on to recommend that, since prostitution is so widespread, we should abolish our laws against it! While I don't agree with his solution, he has certainly appraised the problem accurately. Since Adam and Eve left the Garden of Eden, there have always been some people desperate enough to sell their bodies on the open market. Today prostitution has a more professional look, but its motive is still the same. Men and women still enter prostitution because of financial problems, family pressures, or some other breakdown of normal life. Seldom does a person become a prostitute on a whim. It is a deliberate, often unwilling, step that a person takes. But once a prostitute has started to sell sex, it becomes an accepted way of life; the cycle is hard to break. What does God say about this problem?

*50. Do not prostitute thy daughter, to cause her to be a whore; lest the land fall to whoredom, and the land become full of wickedness. (Lev. 19:29)*

God calls prostitution "wickedness." He does not allow us to send our daughters into prostitution because it is a "wicked" thing to do. Also, the book of Proverbs gives very strict warnings to any man who feels tempted to patronize a prostitute:

*51. Let not thine heart decline to her ways, go not astray in her paths. For she hath cast down many wounded: yea, many strong men have been slain by her. Her house is the way to hell, going down to the chambers of death.*
*(Prov. 7:25–27)*

That's putting it bluntly, isn't it? God says that the prostitute will take you to hell; she will destroy the soul as well as the body. The greatest hazard in visiting a prostitute is not the disease you might contract (although that certainly is a hazard); the greatest danger is that you will lose your soul by corrupting yourself with such a person.

Again, God is ready to forgive a prostitute who repents. He loves the prostitute, and He is ready to cleanse him or her of all the guilt and suffering this sin has created.

Remember the sinful woman who came and knelt at Jesus' feet, washing them with her tears? The people around Jesus criticized Him for associating with her. But He said, *"Her sins, which are many, are forgiven, for she loved much; but he who is forgiven little, loves little"* (Luke 7:47 RSV). Many times a person who has been deep in sin, like the prostitute, becomes one of the most radiant Christians because Christ has forgiven so much. God's promise is sure. He will forgive anyone who is truly sorry for the past. (See Colossians 2:13–14.)

# Bestiality

Now we look at something that will really shock you. Forgive me for even mentioning it, because it is repulsive; but deal with it we must, because God deals with it in His Word.

I am talking about bestiality—having sexual relations with animals. This perversion of sex was much more common in the ancient world than it is today, but some people still practice it. Pornographic movies and magazines use scenes of bestiality for "shock value," and some people decide to experiment with it. God speaks very frankly about this practice:

# Sexual Perversion Bears a Curse

*52. Neither shalt thou lie with any beast to defile thyself therewith: neither shall any woman stand before a beast to lie down thereto: it is confusion.*
*(Lev. 18:23)*

*And if a woman approach unto any beast, and lie down thereto, thou shalt kill the woman, and the beast: they shall surely be put to death; their blood shall be upon them.* *(Lev. 20:16)*

Bestiality is an unspeakable perversion of the divine gift of sex. I can hardly find words to express how sickening this practice is to any decent-minded person, much less to Almighty God. Yet some people do it. Once again we have an example of how sex is cheapened by the carnal mind, how it is considered a plaything for the idle. Bestiality proves how far the ungodly mind will descend into degradation.

## The Freedom and the Curse

When God gave us sex, He gave us the freedom to choose how we would use it. His guidelines are here before us, but He will not force us to follow them. We must decide on our own.

> God cannot deny man the right to do wrong. Such inhibitions would reduce man to the level of animals or insects. The same freedom of choice which permits a man to be noble and compassionate also allows him to be greedy and hateful.[3]

This freedom is the most exhilarating aspect of being a man or woman. A sense of dignity is created that no other creature can know. But when we use that gift to deny the Giver, we have acted very foolishly indeed. We bring upon ourselves the curse of the consequences.

Perhaps you have been caught up in some type of perversion. Perhaps you have fallen prey to the spirit of lust, which leads to frustration, condemnation, depression, and finally death. If so, I have good news for you—Christ can set you free from it. I have prayed for hundreds of people to be delivered from homosexuality, and God has answered in marvelous ways.

Regardless of how faithful you have been to the church, if you are perverting sex you will never enter the kingdom of heaven. That's what God says. Sexual perversion is an insult to God.

But God forgives a sinner who repents. I have seen homosexuals give their lives to the Lord and right away they begin to change; their faces look different and their entire beings take on a different countenance. Men become more masculine and women become more feminine. This is what God's forgiveness can do.

If you have this kind of problem in your family, I urge you to use the Bible as your standard. Find God's final word on sex and sexual perversion, and cast out the perversion in Jesus' holy name.

## Notes

1. Carl C. Williams, *Chicken Coops or Sky Scrapers?* (Anderson, Ind.: Warner, 1973), p. 12.

2. Sanford H. Kadish, "The Crisis of Overcriminalization," *Crime, Criminology, and Contemporary Society*, ed. Richard D. Knudten (Homewood, Ill.: The Dorsey Press, 1970), p. 8.

3. Mort Crim, *Like It Is!* (Anderson, Ind.: Portal Books, 1972), p. 32.

# 8

# The Deceptions of Sex

Joy is often confused with simple pleasure. The joy of
which the Bible speaks fills one from the inside out.

—Cyvette Guerra[1]

S atan can fool you into thinking that sex is the
answer to all your problems, but this is a delusion. In fact, it can be another one of your problems! God wants men and women to live together
and love together in the context of marriage. Since the
beginning of time, though, Satan has tried to deceive
us into using sex for illicit reasons. He has tried to turn
one of Gods greatest gifts to his own advantage. Unfortunately, he has often succeeded.

People who come to me for counseling say, "I
wanted a little extra joy, a little extra excitement from
sex. Instead it turned out to be a nightmare." They are
talking about their illicit use of sex, their desire to try
something different from what God had intended.

Satan has deceived men and women about sex in many ways. Let us examine some of his favorite deceptions.

## Sex Is Not a God

In some parts of the world, sex is worshipped. Two thousand years ago, for example, the people of Ephesus worshipped a sex goddess called Diana who was supposed to have twelve breasts. (See Acts 19.) I have visited the ruins of Diana's temple. Beside the temple was a den of prostitutes; men who came to the temple had sexual relations with the prostitutes as part of their "worship."

In India, I have seen temples to the sex goddess Cali. (The city of Calcutta is named after her.) Worshippers will slit the throat of a goat and let its blood run under the idol of Cali, so that she will allow a woman to conceive a child. They believe that Cali controls the use of sex.

In their own way, many Americans also worship sex. They wear clothing that accentuates their sex organs and arouses the lust of the opposite sex. They read salacious magazines and attend X-rated movies to indulge their restless appetite for stimulation. Women undergo surgery to enlarge their breasts, while men take hormone shots to boost their virility. It's all done in the name of the great god Sex.

Sex is not a god. Sex is a servant of mankind. God designed sex to undergird the unity and happiness of the home, to provide a new generation of men and women. When we are dead and gone, our children and grandchildren will follow us in the long procession of God's people; the gift of sex, insures that the procession will continue.

# The Deceptions of Sex

Sex is a beautiful and holy gift, but it is not to be worshipped.

## Perversion Brings No Satisfaction

Satan tricks many people into thinking that sexual perversion will make them happy. Normal sexual relations do not satisfy them, so they try all sorts of perverted lifestyles in an effort to find what's "right for me."

Entire books have been devoted to the topic of how to have a homosexual affair, how to lure a married man into bed with you, how to practice good hygiene as a prostitute, and so on. These filthy books fill their readers' minds with perverse ideas they would not have gotten otherwise; it is a tragic error even to read them. A healthy, godly person doesn't gain anything from reading literature about abnormal, perverted sex. There is little value in sex manuals that teach all sorts of strange, exotic positions for intercourse. I firmly believe that marriage partners can teach one another much more than they can ever learn from a book. Professor Andrew M. Greeley of the University of Arizona recently said:

> Sophisticated lovers know that in the bedroom or anywhere else gentleness has incredible erotic power. A kiss at the nape of the neck, a contact of two hands, fingers brushing lightly and quickly...all of these subtle actions have much more powerful erotic impact than do the acrobatics and gymnastics of the sex manuals performed without tenderness. If what happens in the marriage bed is not pervaded by gentleness, sexual relations are likely to be both unsatisfying and infrequent.[2]

Sexual perversion and sexual experimentation cannot take the place of honest, open sexual relations between husband and wife. Sex was created for marriage, and that is where it gives the greatest fulfillment.

We also need to keep these things in proper spiritual perspective. God tells us that:

*53. Angels who did not keep their proper domain, but left their own abode, He has reserved in everlasting chains under darkness for the judgment of the great day; as Sodom and Gomorrah,...having given themselves over to sexual immorality and gone after strange flesh, are set forth as an example, suffering the vengeance of eternal fire.* (Jude 6–7 NKJV)

People who pervert sex to "go after strange flesh" are destined to die. God places them in the same pit with the rebellious angels who defied His will in heaven. That's what sexual perversion is—a defiance of God's will. The people of Sodom and Gomorrah were deceived into thinking that prostitution, homosexuality, bestiality, and other perversions were more fun than sexual relations in marriage. But they were destroyed for it! They will be sent to hell for what they did.

You may say, "I don't believe in hell." But that makes no difference. You may not believe the sun will rise tomorrow, but that won't stop it from happening. What you believe has nothing to do with God's enforcing His will. The strands of history are running forward to their inevitable conclusion, and the end will bring judgment upon those who have profaned God's gift of sex.

# The Deceptions of Sex

## Multiple Mating

Satan has deceived many people into thinking that they will enjoy sex more if they have sexual relations with several people. This might be called "multiple mating." We see it expressed in the prostitution, promiscuity, and adultery that stains every level of our society.

In biblical times, the most common form of multiple mating was polygamy—the practice of marrying more than one wife. It was permitted in the Old Testament world; in fact, custom dictated that a wealthy man should have many wives. The first recorded polygamist in the Bible was Lamech (see Genesis 4:23-25); he had two wives. Some men, such as King Solomon, had hundreds of wives. As a missionary in Hong Kong and Manila, I met quite a few polygamous couples. Not one of them was happy. I believe their problems were typical of those anyone in the United States encounters in multiple mating, even though it's practiced differently here.

No woman wants to receive half a man's love and no man wants to receive half of hers. True love—especially when it is expressed sexually—is a total giving of oneself to someone else. It isn't something that gets more enjoyable as you "spread it around."

Yet God's Word says that we can expect more multiple mating as we approach the final judgment. Read what He says through the prophet Isaiah:

*54. And in that day seven women shall take hold of one man, saying, We will eat our own bread, and wear our own apparel: only let us be called by thy name, to take away our reproach.*

*(Isa. 4:1)*

As we approach the end of time, people will become more desperate for sexual fulfillment. During the great Tribulation, which will precede the Lord's return, wars and famine will ravage the male population. There will be fewer men to act as fathers. So several women will go to a man and say, "Give us children. You don't have to support us, you don't even have to love us—just help us conceive children. We can't bear the shame of being barren." They will try multiple mating, and they will find sex to be less fulfilling than ever. That's what God predicts.

# A Price to Pay

Have you ever seen people play "the old shell game"? It seems very simple. Someone places a pea under one of three walnut shells, then shuffles the shells back and forth across the tabletop. The object is to guess which shell has the pea under it. But no one can. The operator's hand is "quicker than the eye," and he can trick you into thinking the pea is where it isn't.

That's exactly what Satan tries to do with sex. He tries to trick us into thinking that real joy and satisfaction are found in lust, carnality, and perversion. But it just isn't true. These are deviations from the sex life God intended us to have; they will bring us nothing but deformed bodies, feeble minds, unsatisfied desires, and slavery to sin.

Don't get caught in Satan's "shell game." Listen to what God tells you about sex, and you will find the satisfaction you long for.

# The Deceptions of Sex

# Notes

1. Cyvette Guerra, *The Joy Robbers* (Nashville: Impact, 1979), p. 10.

2. Andrew M. Greeley, "To Increase the Enjoyment of Sex in Marriage," *Reader's Digest*, September 1978, p. 113.

# 9

# How Jesus Dealt with Sex Offenders

If I close down, there'll be another porno movie house
open tomorrow. Look, you can't tell other people what's
for them....These creeps come in here and masturbate or
worse while the picture's on. But so what?
It's a free country....

—A theater manager[1]

Jesus Christ cares about what is happening to the
sex morals of our world. During His earthly ministry in Palestine, He often confronted people who
indulged in adultery, prostitution, and other kinds of
sexual perversion. He criticized the Pharisees for being
too lenient about divorce. He explained what creates
a happy, harmonious life in every respect—including
sex.

As we study Jesus' dealings with sex offenders, we
find that He used loving firmness to call people back
to the proper use of sex. This gives us valuable insights

into Jesus' overall teachings about sex. We see how deeply Jesus cares about our sex life.

We find a good example of Jesus' concern for sex offenders in John 8, which tells how the scribes and Pharisees brought to Him a woman they had caught in the act of adultery. Scripture tells us that they had taken her *"in the very act"* of having adulterous intercourse with another man (v. 4). There was no question about her guilt since they had seen her sin firsthand. After bringing the adulteress to Jesus, the men reminded Him that God's law required them to stone such a person. "What do you say?" they asked.

Notice that they weren't interested in the woman; they were interested in proving a point of law. As far as they were concerned, she was just another case, an exhibit for "Show and Tell" at their Pharisaic law school. They couldn't care less whether she lived or died; testing Jesus on a point of law interpretation was their entire purpose.

Jesus could see through all of that. He said, *"He who is without sin among you, let him throw a stone at her first"* (v. 7 NKJV). He didn't question the law; He didn't deny the Scripture. He knew that His heavenly Father had given the law against adultery for a good reason, to prevent a total breakdown of marriage. But He also knew that arguing the case with His enemies would not achieve what the law intended; it would not restore the woman's marriage or protect anyone else's. So Jesus focused on the real problem—the Pharisees' cold, impersonal attitude about sex. The eminent Bible scholar Raymond E. Brown develops this further:

> Jesus...recognized that, although they are zealous for the word of the Law, they are not interested in the purpose of the Law, for the, spiritual

state of the woman is not even in question, or whether or not she is penitent.[2]

God is always just, but loving; He always condemns sin, but forgives the sinner who repents. The Pharisees were too narrow-minded to see that. They could only shake their heads and walk away. And Jesus told the woman, *"Go, and sin no more"* (John 8:11).

Only Jesus Christ could forgive sex offenders like that. Only He could see beyond the sin and shame that covered their lives to uncover the child of God within— the person who was hungry for love. Jesus knew what was happening inside a person's life. We see this again in His Sermon on the Mount:

*55. You have heard that it was said to those of old, "You shall not commit adultery." But I say to you that whoever looks at a woman to lust for her has already committed adultery with her in his heart.*  (Matt. 5:27–28 NKJV)

That's a strong statement, but it shows us once again that Jesus looks at the inward life; He teaches inward strength and godliness. No matter how pure and godly you may seem, if you think lustful thoughts you are guilty of lust.

Lust is common in our world today. Men sit on benches outside the supermarkets and watch the women stroll by, thinking to themselves, "Man, wouldn't I like to have her! Wouldn't I like to take her to bed!" These men do not realize that they are sinning against God just by thinking that. They are toying with the idea of infidelity. They are entertaining Satan's delusions.

Jesus said that adultery is not just a physical act; it is a defilement of the heart. If you wish to do it—even if you think about doing it—you have already betrayed your true sex partner. You are just as guilty of adultery as if you had paid for an overnight motel room and taken the woman with you. Jesus Christ judges you for what you really are.

Satan will try to plant evil ideas in your mind; no matter how righteous you are, Satan will tempt you to lust after the opposite sex. Whenever that happens, start to pray. You can say, "Lord, take it away. I don't want to be that kind of person. I'm not a carnal person on the outside, and I don't want to be carnal on the inside. So take that thought out of my mind." You know what will happen? The Lord will make you clean again.

Joseph confronted this kind of problem. His master, Potiphar, placed him in charge of his house and all his possessions while he was away on business. Potiphar's wife began to lust after Joseph, and one day she said, *"Lie with me"* (Gen. 39:7). It would have been so easy for Joseph to give in. He could have rationalized his sin and said, "Oh, well, I'd better do what my master's wife says!" But Joseph knew this was nothing more than lust, and he put it right out of his mind. *"How then can I do this great wickedness,"* he said, *"and sin against God?"* (v. 9).

Joseph realized that lust was not simply a sin against Potiphar or Potiphar's wife—it was a sin against God! It insulted the Lord of his life. It offended the One who made Joseph's sex drive. Regardless of how pleasurable it might have seemed for the moment, Joseph knew this affair was a "great wickedness," and he put it out of his mind. Potiphar's wife kept trying to seduce him, but he kept turning his back on the temptation. Finally, she grabbed his clothes to pull him into her bed. Joseph tore out of his clothes and ran away!

Now that's what I call fleeing temptation!

## How to Avoid the Offense

Satan will get you into embarrassing situations like that, and you will have to decide what to do. He will test your morals. He will try to destroy you. But Christ teaches us to resist Satan every step of the way.

We can resist Satan's temptations in several ways. First, we can avoid situations that might get us into trouble. I have been in the ministry for quite a few years, and I have learned never to be alone with a woman who might ask me to go to bed with her. That way I give the devil no chance to do his dirty work. I deal with people openly, honestly, and straightforwardly. My ministry is clean because I don't let Satan get his foot in the door.

Second, we can avoid temptation by keeping our thoughts where they ought to be. The prophet Isaiah said, *"Thou wilt keep him in perfect peace, whose mind is stayed on thee"* (Isa. 26:3). It's difficult for Satan to break through that kind of relationship; he has a hard time turning our thoughts to lust if we are meditating on God and His will. Jesus followed this course when Satan tried to tempt him in the wilderness. (See Matthew 4.) Every time Satan started to whisper in His ear, Jesus turned His thoughts to Scripture. The moment Satan started to say, "Think how much fun it would be to do such and such," Jesus bounced it back to him with the Word of God. Try that the next time you are tempted.

Third, we can resist temptation by putting our lives in the eternal perspective. By that I mean we should constantly think about the eternal consequences of what we are doing. We should always ask ourselves, "Is this going to make me any happier in heaven?" Believe me, that throws cold water on any wild impulses. When

Satan lulls you into fuzzy thinking about sex, that one question can snap you back to reality.

Jesus did this on at least one occasion. He put marriage and sex in eternal perspective, saying, *"In the resurrection they neither marry, nor are given in marriage, but are as the angels of God in heaven"* (Matt. 22:30).

There will be no sexual relations in heaven; there will be no procreating of children there. Why? Because everyone will be like angels. Our immortality will make reproduction unnecessary. Everyone's enjoyment of the presence of the Son of God will take away the need for physical pleasures. The purpose of sex will be ended, just as the purpose of marriage will be ended. In that light, any thoughts about multiple mating seem very foolish indeed.

As the old gospel song says, "This world is not my home; I'm just a-passin' through." Sex and marriage seem terribly urgent now, but they have very little value in the eternal scheme of things. I'm not making light of sex and marriage. To the contrary, God says that our behavior in this area will affect whether we go to heaven or hell. But Christ says that gratifying our sexual desires is not all-important. While we think the world revolves around sex and marriage, Christ sees the end of the world. He says, *"Heaven and earth will pass away,"*—yes, even sex will pass away—*"but My words will by no means pass away"* (Matt. 24:35 NKJV). A. W. Tozer gave this graphic description of the attitude many Christians have toward the present, physical life:

> Men think of the world, not as a battleground but as a playground. We are not here to fight, we are here to frolic. We are not in a foreign land, we are at home. We are not getting ready to live,

we are already living, and the best we can do is rid ourselves of our inhibitions and our frustrations and live this life to the full. This, we believe, is a fair summary of the religious philosophy of modern man.[3]

But this is a delusion! We are not at home in this present world. We are not entitled to look after our own comfort while the rest of the world goes to hell. We are on assignment here; we have a mission to fulfill for the Lord. There are many things more important than working through our sexual frustrations and fantasies. Our sexual hang-ups will mean nothing in eternity, because there will be no sex in eternity. When we hold this fact firmly in mind, sexual temptation loses its allure.

## Forgiveness for Offenders

While we are thinking about Jesus' teachings on sex, we should take special note of the way He forgave sex offenders. He shows us once again that God is ready to welcome back anyone who repents of sin—even a sexual sin.

When Jesus traveled through the region of Samaria, He stopped at a well to get a drink. A woman came to dip her jar in the well, and Jesus struck up a conversation with her. This was highly unusual because Jews had a deep resentment of the Samaritans, who were a mixed breed, half-Jew and half-Gentile. But Jesus was so interested in this woman's soul that He didn't let racial differences stand in the way. He talked to her. And after discussing theology for a few minutes, Jesus said, *"Go, call your husband, and come here"* (John 4:16 NKJV).

The woman must have smiled as she said, *"I have no husband"* (v. 17 NKJV).

*"You have well said, 'I have no husband,'"* Jesus replied, *"for you have had five husbands, and the one whom you now have is not your husband; in that you spoke truly"* (v. 17–18 NKJV).

Notice that Jesus did not condemn her for her sin. He did not shame her for what she had done. But He did confront her with the truth; He told her pointblank that her sex life needed to be straightened out. He let her know that He was well aware of her promiscuous life, and He wanted her to "come clean" before God.

Earlier I mentioned the incident in which a woman anointed Jesus' feet with tears (Luke 7:36–50). The Bible simply says that she was *"a woman in the city who was a sinner"* (v. 37 NKJV). The Bible commentator Charles L. Childers says, "Such an expression as this, in New Testament terminology, means a prostitute."[4] Dr. Childers' interpretation seems confirmed by the way the Pharisees reacted to this woman. They said, *"This man, if He were a prophet, would know who and what manner of woman this is who is touching Him, for she is a sinner"* (v. 39 NKJV).

The Pharisees were careful students of the Law. They did not want to defile themselves by touching anyone who had violated God's commandments. So they would have nothing to do with the woman.

But observe Jesus' attitude. He watched her kneel at His feet and weep unashamedly in front of all the men; then she let down her long hair and used it to wipe His feet, washing them with her tears. Jesus had compassion on her. He could see through her sin of prostitution and discern the needs of her heart. So He said, *"Your sins are forgiven....Your faith has saved you. Go in peace"* (vv. 48, 50 NKJV). The master expositor Matthew Henry writes:

# How Jesus Dealt with Sex Offenders

> Let who will object, Christ will bid the peni-
> tent that applies to him depart in peace, partak-
> ing of salvation through faith in his name. But
> may we not with shame confess, that while we
> hope our offenses are freely pardoned, we love
> but little?...Instead of grudging greater sinners the
> mercy they find with Christ, upon their repen-
> tance, we should be stirred up by their example
> to examine ourselves, whether we are indeed for-
> given, and do love Christ.[5]

This is God's grace at work. By no means do we see
Jesus treat sexual offenses in a casual, halfhearted way.
He takes sin seriously, but He also takes repentance
seriously. Whenever a sex offender comes to Him and
says, "Lord, I'm sorry for what I've done," Jesus is ready
to forgive. He is ready to forget the offense of the prostitute, the adulterer, the homosexual, or the person guilty
of any other sexual offense. Sexual sins are very grave
matters in God's sight; but He is just as willing to forgive the sex offender as He is to forgive the "smallest"
sin of a godly person.

Christ can make "something beautiful" of your life.
No matter what your sins have been—even if you have
been sexually immoral in the vilest way—Jesus stands
ready to forgive you and cleanse you of your sin. He
can wipe the evil deeds and evil thoughts out of your
life forever, if you give Him a chance.

## Notes

1. Paul Moore and Joe Musser, *Shepherd of Times Square*
(Nashville: Thomas Nelson, 1979), p. 152.

2. Raymond E. Brown, *The Anchor Bible*, vol. 29 (Garden City,
N.Y.: Doubleday, 1966), p. 388.

3. Warren W. Wiersbe, ed., *The Best of A. W. Tozer* (Grand Rapids, Mich.: Baker, 1978), pp. 85–86.

4. Charles L. Childers, "The Gospel according to Luke," *Beacon Bible Commentary*, vol. 6, ed. A. F. Harper (Kansas City: Beacon Hill, 1964), p. 485.

5. Matthew Henry and Thomas Scott, *Commentary on the Holy Bible*, vol. 3 (Nashville: Thomas Nelson, 1979), pp. 247–48.

# 10
# Sex and Spiritual Reality

Under the figures of the tenderest affection...the Divine
love is represented [in the Book of Hosea] as ever
enduring in spite of all indifference and opposition;
and, on the other hand, the waywardness, unblushing
faithlessness of the loved one is painted in colors so
repulsive as almost to shock the moral sense.

—James Robertson[1]

The Bible uses sex to portray the deepest spiritual
truths. God has some very practical things to say
about sex; this is because God is intensely interested in our well being and happiness, and He knows
that sex is a vital part of our happiness. But we would
be shortchanging ourselves if we did not notice the
spiritual side of God's Word on sex. He uses sexual
symbols to convey some of the most stunning pictures
of the gospel.

The relationship between a person's sex life and his or her spiritual life also needs to be pursued further. This is one of the most misunderstood aspects of human sexuality. The popular sex manuals would have us believe that sexual fulfillment is simply a matter of biology or emotions; but it is also a matter of the spirit. If you are not in harmony with the God who made you a sexual creature, you cannot expect to be in harmony with your sex partner. Besides that, sex can affect your spiritual growth.

## Sex as a Spiritual Symbol

The Bible often uses marriage, adultery, prostitution, and other sex-related acts to illustrate spiritual truth. Perhaps the best-known example of this is found in the book of Hosea. Here the prophet Hosea is told to marry a prostitute in order to illustrate God's love for His rebellious people. The result is one of the most bizarre yet beautiful stories of the entire Bible.

*And the LORD said to Hosea, Go, take unto thee a wife of whoredoms and children of whoredoms: for the land hath committed great whoredom, departing from the LORD.* (Hos. 1:2)

Imagine what Hosea's neighbors thought of this course of action. A handsome young prophet marries a prostitute and says, "The Lord told me to do it." I suspect his friends said, "Ha! That's what he says! I wonder what the real story is."

But God had indeed told Hosea to marry this "woman of the night." He commanded the preacher to become a living example of how God was going to treat the wayward nation of Israel. Preachers can have some very tough assignments, but I can't imagine a more difficult calling than Hosea had. God made Hosea and his wife Gomer an object lesson for the entire nation. Hosea was able to tell his people, "Look! You have made yourselves prostitutes with all sorts of pagan gods, just as Gomer made herself a prostitute with other men. But God loves you and will forgive you, just like I forgave Gomer and married her."

Gomer proved unfaithful again. After she bore children to Hosea, she left home and became the concubine of another man. Hosea corrected her and purchased her from the other man, bringing her back into his home once again. He never stopped loving her, despite her unfaithfulness. As one commentator notes, his love for her was "a beautiful equilibrium of loving tenderness and severe judgment."[2]

I cannot think of a more dramatic way to describe how God loves us and redeems us from our unfaithfulness to Him. When a husband forgives an adulterous wife and brings her back into his home, that's true forgiveness and love.

We find another stunning sex-related spiritual symbol in Revelation 17, where John sees a vision of a great harlot riding on a scarlet-colored beast. John said:

> *The woman was arrayed in purple and scarlet, and adorned with gold and precious stones and pearls, having in her hand a golden cup full of abominations and the filthiness of her fornication. And on her forehead a name was written: MYSTERY, BABYLON THE GREAT, THE MOTHER OF HARLOTS AND OF ABOMINATIONS OF THE EARTH. I saw the woman, drunk with the blood of the saints and with the blood of the martyrs of Jesus.*
>
> (Rev. 17:4–6 NKJV)

This is a vision of what will happen at the end time, just before Christ returns to earth. John said that at the end time a profane and sinful power will arise upon the earth, like a great harlot, who will wreak havoc upon the church of Jesus Christ. This sinful power will kill saints by the thousands; it will all but wipe out Christianity as we know it today. The figure of the harlot is a striking contrast to the bride of Christ—the faithful church that will consummate her love with Christ at the end of time. (See Revelation 21:9–21.) Indeed, I believe the harlot symbolizes an unfaithful church, a church that prostitutes itself by following other lords besides Christ. The harlot stands for a "world church" inspired by Satan himself, which will ally itself with the Antichrist and blaspheme the holy name of Jesus. This "world church" will deny the Virgin Birth. It will deny the miracles of Jesus; in fact, it will deny the Bible itself. Giving itself to all kinds of unclean practices, it will ride upon the system of the Antichrist, the Beast. God calls this unfaithful church a harlot because she will sell her soul to the devil.

My friend, terrible times are coming to this earth. As we will see in the next chapter, we are about to enter a time of great suffering and tribulation that leads up to the return of Jesus. Many people won't survive. Many Christians will fall away from the Lord. Unbelievers will cast their lot with the unfaithful church, the "great whore," instead of following Jesus. And they will be destroyed in the end. We ought to pay careful attention to these sex-related symbols, because God can use them to teach crucial lessons to us.

Another sex-related symbol of the end time is found in Matthew 25, where Jesus describes what will happen just before He returns. He says that the kingdom of heaven will be like ten virgins waiting for their prospective husband. Five of the virgins are wise; they buy a generous supply of oil to last through the night, so they will be sure to have their lamps burning when the young man comes. But the other five virgins are foolish, because they let their lamps burn with a meager supply of oil, hoping that the young man will come soon.

The night wears on, and the young man is delayed. At midnight they hear an attendant shouting, *"Behold, the bridegroom cometh; go ye out to meet him"* (v. 6).

Suddenly the five foolish virgins realize that their lamps are out of oil. They beg the five wise virgins to give them some. But they answer, *"Not so; lest there be not enough for us and you"* (v. 9). Then the five foolish virgins rush down to the lamp shop and buy a fresh supply of oil, while their five friends go into the banquet hall with the eligible young bachelor. When the five foolish virgins return, the banquet hall is locked; they pound on the door and shout to be let in. But the young man says, *"Verily I say unto you, I know you not"* (v. 12). (Perhaps he thinks they are prostitutes, for what other kind of woman would be roaming the streets at night?)

The moral of the story, Jesus said, is that we must always be ready to receive Him. No one knows when Christ will return to earth to claim His people.

Notice once again how vividly God has illustrated this spiritual truth by using the symbol of sex. A virgin is an unmarried woman who keeps herself free from illicit sex. She has not indulged in premarital sex or promiscuous flirting; she has kept herself pure for the man she knows will someday ask her to marry him. In the same way, Jesus says, we should keep ourselves spiritually pure until He returns to claim us for His own.

## Sex and Your Spiritual Life

We could examine several other examples of how God used sex to drive home a spiritual message. The Bible is full of such passages, and the ones I have cited just give you a taste of them. For now, though, let us think about the link between sex and your own spiritual life. How does your sexual behavior affect your relationship with God?

Even in Old Testament times, God showed His people that their sex life and their spiritual life affected one another. This connection is why God laid down so many regulations concerning marriage, why he was so protective in matters of adultery and promiscuity. He gave men and women the gift of sex for wholesome and holy reasons, and He did not want to see it profaned. Moreover, He knew that a wayward sex life would lead a person to dishonor God in other areas; it would be the first step toward wholesale spiritual decay. So God regulated the conduct of a person's sex life with great care.

The book of Leviticus contains some very interesting laws that reveal the tie-in between the sexual and the spiritual. For example, Leviticus 15 prohibits a man from worshipping at the temple if he has recently had sexual intercourse or if he has touched a woman during her menstrual period:

*56. And if any man's seed of copulation go out from him, then he shall wash all his flesh in water, and be unclean until the even. And every garment, and every skin, whereon is the seed of copulation, shall be washed with water, and be unclean until the even. The woman also with*

*whom man shall lie with seed of copulation,
they shall both bathe themselves in water, and
be unclean until the even. And if a woman have
an issue, and her issue in her flesh be blood,
she shall be put apart seven days: and whosoever
toucheth her shall be unclean until the even.*
(Lev. 15:16–19)

Scholars argue about what this passage means;
surely it cannot mean that these natural processes are
evil. I think it shows that God expected a person to
spend some time in meditation and prayer, preparing
for worship before actually coming into the house of
God, and God knew that a person who was overly concerned with physical things could not worship Him
wholeheartedly.

Perhaps Matthew Henry's comment is also helpful
at this point. He says, "These laws remind us that God
sees all things, even those which are concealed from
human eyes, and escape the censures of men."[3] As we
have been saying all along, God makes no separation
between a person's physical and spiritual life: Both are
part of the same life. Anything that you do sexually
will affect every other aspect of your life, including
your worship. God wants to keep you mindful of that.

In Paul's letters, he often warns the early Christians
to keep their sex lives pure because of the effect this
will have on their spiritual lives. Here is such a warning from Paul's first letter to the Corinthians:

*57. Flee sexual immorality. Every sin that a man
does is outside the body, but he who commits
sexual immorality sins against his own body. Or
do you not know that your body is the temple of*

*the Holy Spirit who is in you, whom you have
from God, and you are not your own? For you
were bought at a price; therefore glorify God in
your body and in your spirit, which are God's.*
(1 Cor. 6:18–20 NKJV)

Many of us have memorized verse 19, which says,
*"Do you not know that your body is the temple of the Holy
Spirit...and you are not your own?"* I have heard this verse
quoted to condemn cigarette smoking, drug abuse, and
drinking. All of those are valid applications—but the
original application was to sex! God tells us that our
bodies are holy temples where He can live and reign;
but we defile these temples if we indulge in promiscuity. Loose living exposes our bodies to venereal disease and infection leading to heart disease, blindness,
or insanity. To put it bluntly, *promiscuity can destroy the
temple of God.* It can ruin any chance we have to serve
God with our physical bodies. So promiscuity raises
both a physical danger and a spiritual danger, dem-
onstrating once again that sexuality and spirituality
cannot be neatly broken apart.

Anyone who lives a life of sexual perversion cannot
be a victorious Christian. That should be obvious. A
prostitute does not glorify Christ by the way he or she
lives; a homosexual does not honor the Lord with the
temple of his or her body. You do not have to be a
theologian to realize that. Any practice that abuses or
corrupts the bodies God has given us is a shame and
mockery to the gospel. It cuts off the testimony that
a person could otherwise give to the Lord. Christians
must purge them out of their lives; they must get rid of
any sexual deviancy or sin in order to live lives that are
holy unto the Lord.

## Moral Lawlessness

Sexual immorality has spiritual consequences for nations as well. Ungodly people make an ungodly nation, and God will not fail to punish a nation that turns away from Him. D. Elton Trueblood pointed this out in his book entitled *Foundations for Reconstruction,* written just after World War II.

> Sexual corruption is one of the chief symptoms of a sick and decaying society. The right ordering of the relations between the sexes is so important to a culture that any culture which fails to deal realistically with the problem is likely to go to pieces.[4]

Isn't that what we see in America today? Families are breaking up, businesses are falling apart, and the government itself is sliding into graft and corruption because of immoral sex and the selfish attitudes that accompany it. We live in a hedonistic age that defies the moral laws of almighty God. But no one can revoke God's laws. The sexual deviant, the prostitute, and the adulterer don't negate Gods law—they simply illustrate it. Their stories will not be finished until the day of reckoning when Christ returns.

Several years ago, when I was a missionary to South America, I lived on a compound with eight or ten other missionary families. One of the women was an incurable socialite; in common parlance, she was a "rounder." I think this woman went to every party within driving distance of our mission station. She was rarely around her cottage because she spent most of her waking hours gallivanting around town in her husband's jeep "looking for action." To be honest, she was not a very spiritual person, and I suspected that she had some habits that were very unbecoming to a Christian.

One day this lady became ill and sent word for me to come and pray for her. I replied that I was busy and could not come. Again she sent a message for me to come, and again I declined. Finally, her husband came and said, "Aren't you going to come and pray?"

"Yes, I will," I said. "But I'm in no hurry."

"Why not?" he asked.

"I've been holding revival meetings for several days, and I have yet to see her in church," I said.

"But she's been busy!"

"Brother," I said, "your wife has been doing ungodly things with ungodly people and living an ungodly way of life in town instead of going to church. Do you think that just because she snaps her fingers I ought to jump?"

My friend didn't expect that. He walked away with a dazed look on his face.

At last I went to the woman's bedside. She said, "Oh, thank goodness you're here! Pray for me, Brother Sumrall. Pray for me!"

"No," I said, "I would rather talk to you. Why haven't you been in church?"

"Oh, I've been so busy I just haven't had time to come," she said. "Maybe I've been a little bit too busy."

"Well, it looks to me like you intend to stay too busy," I replied. "God has put you where you won't be so busy."

"Aren't you going to pray for me?"

"Yes, I'll pray with you after I finish talking with you," I said. "Are you ready to repent of your sins?"

She didn't answer.

"Are you ready to ask for God's forgiveness? Are you?"

# Sex and Spiritual Reality

Tears welled up in her eyes, and I could tell she was finally facing up to her sinfulness. "Yes," she said, "I want to repent. I'm sorry for what I've done."

So I led her in a sinner's prayer, asking God to forgive her sins. Then I laid my hand on her forehead and prayed earnestly that God would make her whole again. The Spirit of the Lord moved mightily, and I could feel His power flowing into her body. She was healed within the hour!

You cannot escape God's moral law, no matter how "slick" you are. The day will come when you must admit all of the sins—even the secret, sexual sins—standing between you and God.

## Your Spiritual Life and Sex

Yes, the sexual life can affect the spiritual life; but the reverse is also true. Sex is predominantly a spiritual thing, and the breakthrough for sex problems often begins with prayer.

We find a touching example of this in the Old Testament, which tells how a woman named Hannah went to the temple and prayed that God would let her conceive a son. Her husband had another wife who bore him children, but Hannah was barren; the Bible tells us that the other wife *"provoked her sore, for to make her fret, because the LORD had shut up her womb"* (1 Sam. 1:6). The Israelites believed that God controlled a person's sex life; they trusted Him to bless their marriages with children, and they saw barrenness as a curse. So Hannah wept and prayed that God would give her a child. Here is what happened:

> *And they* [Hannah and her husband] *rose up in the morning early, and worshipped before the LORD,*

*and returned, and came to their house to Ramah: and Elkanah knew Hannah his wife; and the LORD remembered her. Wherefore it came to pass, when the time was come about after Hannah had conceived, that she bare a son, and called his name Samuel, saying, Because I have asked him of the LORD.* (1 Sam. 1:19–20)

Millions of women have received children in this same way. They know that sex is God-given, that children themselves are God-given, so they are not ashamed to bring their request to the Lord. I have personally prayed for many women who could not conceive, and God has allowed them to bear children. I know that a person's relationship with the Lord can affect his or her sexual life.

If you face a sexual problem that seems to have no solution, take heart—God can work a miracle for you! He can free you from inhibitions and fears about sex. He can take away the lustful desire to engage in illicit sexual relationships. He can give you the ability to have children, to enjoy sex with your mate, to become a better sexual partner yourself. He can do all these things because your sex life is all wrapped up with your spiritual life.

But be careful not to let sex become the chief purpose of your life. It's important to remember that sex is a gift, not a goal; it is a way station, not the Way. The chief goal and purpose of your life should be to honor and glorify the Lord.

Sometimes it is even necessary to abstain from sex to realize that goal. We find this in one of God's instructions to married couples:

*58. Do not deprive one another except with consent for a time, that you may give yourselves*

# Sex and Spiritual Reality

*to fasting and prayer; and come together again*
*so that Satan does not tempt you because of your*
*lack of self-control.*               *(1 Cor. 7:5 NKJV)*

In other words, there may be times when a couple decides to abstain from sexual relations to devote themselves to a season of prayer about a special concern. This does not mean that sex is evil, just as fasting does not mean that eating is evil. This kind of abstinence simply means that a person is willing to put aside the normal functions of the body for a short time, in order to concentrate more completely on prayer and meditation. This is a good discipline, but like fasting, it should only be done for a limited time. Just as a prolonged fast can destroy the body, prolonged continence can destroy a marriage.

While we are on this subject, you might be interested in the reasoning behind the Roman Catholic rule of celibacy. As you know, the Catholic Church does not permit its priests, nuns, or monks to marry. Many of them live in monasteries or convents, virtually cut off from contact with the opposite sex. You might think this is because the Catholic Church thinks sex is evil; but just the opposite is true. In fact, a little research shows that this custom grows out of a deep respect for the sexual relationship in marriage. Catholics follow the rule of celibacy because they know that sex should demand the full commitment of a marriage partner. Pope Pius XII explained it in these terms:

> For the duty of the married life...clearly demands: "They shall be two in one flesh." For spouses are to be bound to each other by mutual bonds both in joy and in sorrow. It is easy to see, therefore, why persons who desire to consecrate

themselves to God's service embrace the state of virginity as a liberation, in order to be more entirely at God's disposition and devoted to the good of their neighbor.[5]

I am not a Catholic and I certainly don't agree with Catholic dogma, but I find this statement extremely fascinating. It affirms the fact that sex demands a one hundred percent commitment of a person's life. Catholic Church leaders abstain from sexual relations all the time to be sure that they are not distracted from God's work, because they know that sex and the spirit are interrelated.

Sex is indeed a one hundred percent commitment. It involves every bit of a person's character. If you want to have a healthy sexual relationship, you can't just think of sex in terms of biology. Think in terms of psychology, because of the involvement of the emotions. Think in terms of philosophy, because of the involvement of the mind. And think in terms of the Bible, because of the involvement of the soul. Sex causes two persons to commune with one another on the deepest levels of their being—and commune with God at the same time.

## Notes

1. James Robertson, "Hosea," *International Standard Bible Encyclopedia*, vol. 3, ed. James Orr et. al. (Grand Rapids, Mich.: Eerdmans, 1939), p. 1426.

2. Francis Davison, ed., *The New Bible Commentary* (Grand Rapids, Mich.: Eerdmans, 1954), p. 682.

3. Matthew Henry and Thomas Scott, *Commentary on the Holy Bible*, vol. 1 (Nashville: Thomas Nelson, 1979), p. 260.

4. D. Elton Trueblood, *Foundations for Reconstruction*, rev. ed. (Waco. Tex.: Word, 1972), p. 71.

5. Anne Fremantle, *The Papal Encyclicals in Their Historical Context* (New York: Mentor-Omega, 1963), p. 301.

# 11
# Sex and the Last Days

At a time in history when standards of conduct are
at an all time low, and when the barriers of holiness
are being broken down by licentiousness, impurity, and
sexual irregularities, Christians ought to rise to the chal-
lenge of living for God in such a way that the world will
know they are true followers of Jesus Christ.

—Harold Lindsell[1]

I have felt deeply impressed to prepare these studies
on sex at the present time. Never before have Christian morals been under such heavy attack. Lewd-
ness and immorality are paraded before our eyes every
day—in bookstores, on television, even on public streets.
Sociologists tell us that our country has experienced a
sexual revolution and so we can expect radical changes
in the way we use sex. But God sheds a different light
on the subject. According to His Word, the profligate
sexual lifestyles of our day are a signal that His Son,
Jesus Christ, is about to return and judge the world.
You can read it in your Bible:

*59. And as it was in the days of Noah, so it will be also in the days of the Son of Man: they ate, they drank, they married wives, they were given in marriage, until the day that Noah entered the ark, and the flood came and destroyed them all. Likewise as it was also in the days of Lot: They ate, they drank, they bought, they sold, they planted, they built; but on the day that Lot went out of Sodom it rained fire and brimstone from heaven and destroyed them all. Even so will it be in the day when the Son of Man is revealed.*
(*Luke 17:26–30 NKJV*)

Think about this for a moment. Think of the situation in our land today and compare it to the world of Noah's day. Compare it to the atmosphere of Sodom and Gomorrah just before God rained His judgment down. Do you see any similarities?

My friend, we are living in those last days. We are about to see the Lord Jesus Christ return to gather His people. I want you to be ready for His coming. I want your life to be pure and holy in God's sight, so that He will look at you and say, *"Well done, thou good and faithful servant"* (Matt. 25:21).

The sinners of Noah's day did not give up their sin, even though Noah warned that God would destroy their world. The homosexuals and prostitutes of Sodom paid no attention to their godly neighbors like Lot until it was too late to change their ways. And so it is today. The people who pervert sex just laugh at their Christian friends; they ridicule what God is trying to tell them. They boast about their "newfound freedom" and encourage other people to join them, tempting even Christians to adopt their wayward lifestyles.

# Sex and the Last Days

Remember Lot's wife. She was being delivered from the terrible judgment God poured out on Sodom and Gomorrah, but at the last minute she looked back. Curious to see what would become of her sinful neighbors, she wondered whether they really would be punished as harshly as God said. She looked back longingly. She became a pillar of salt.

Let me say it again—we are living in the last days. So don't contaminate yourself with the sins of this world. Do not study them with idle curiosity. Do not cozy up to illicit sex and say, "Maybe it's not so bad." Sin is always bad. Sin will destroy you. God says, *"The wages of sin is death"* (Rom. 6:23), and that's the price you can expect to pay for immoral sex.

> *60. But know this, that in the last days perilous times will come: For men will be lovers of themselves, lovers of money, boasters, proud,... lovers of pleasure rather than lovers of God, having a form of godliness but denying its power. And from such people turn away!*
>
> *(2 Tim. 3:1–2, 4–5 NKJV)*

*"Lovers of themselves....lovers of pleasure rather than lovers of God."* How well that describes many people of our day! Self-centered and self-loving, they think that sex is just an exercise in self-gratification. But despite all these efforts to build up the self, they are more lonely and dissatisfied with life than anyone has ever been. They have found exotic sex to be just as disappointing as all the other popular "ego trips." In the process their lives have become a pathetic waste.

Ironically, many pleasure-seekers go through life *"having a form of godliness but denying its power."* They go to church on Sunday and sing "Amazing Grace," but their way of life denies that God has done anything amazing to them. The search for fulfillment is in sex, in drugs, in high-minded learning, or in any number of other things, but it is futile. God predicted this course of events. He foretold in His Word that the pleasure-seeking unbelievers would become more and more dissatisfied as we approach the end of time. That prophecy is coming true right now.

Millions of Americans are living in immorality. Sociologists tell us that half of the brides who walk down the wedding aisle today are not virgins; they have had premarital sex. About ninety percent of young men have engaged in premarital sex. To put it in biblical terms, these men and women have committed fornication. Then they wonder why marriage disappoints them. In the words of Jesus, they *"do not know the Scriptures nor the power of God"* (Mark 12:24 NKJV). They have not listened to what God says about sex.

We can expect things to get worse. Our society will slide into gross immorality and people will take for granted their right to live in perversion. Do not be surprised if Satan's agents get "gay rights" written into the Constitution. Do not be surprised if they start selling do-it-yourself abortion kits. Do not be surprised if they make intercourse a required "final exam" for high-school sex education courses. Such things seem wild and fanciful now, but who would have thought twenty years ago that hospitals would have to give teenage girls abortions on demand? Our nation's sexual morals are on a long downhill slide, and they will slide faster as we get nearer to the time of the Lord's return.

The end of the age will manifest these qualities in worse ways than has been done so far.

# Sex and the Last Days

This is why the Christian does not for a moment believe that men are getting better or that a golden age is around the corner. For the people of God these developments should not be looked upon as a misfortune, although they will suffer grievously. Rather, they should regard them as a sign of hope portending the soon return of the Lord. They are to look up, for their redemption draws near—indeed, it may be nearer than men think![2]

Dr. Lindsell is right. The rotting moral fiber of our time reminds us Christians that our deliverance is almost here. Our Savior is about to return. We are about to consummate the most glorious spiritual event that sex represents—the union of Christ with His bride, the church. It will be the happiest "wedding" this universe has ever known. It will bring us together with Christ in true intimacy and commitment, and we will know firsthand the love that human marriage has foreshadowed for all these centuries. Then sex will pass away. Immorality will pass away. Marriage will pass away as we go to live and reign with Christ.

Are you ready to meet the Lord, or are you one of the sinful signs of His coming? Are you ready to inherit the kingdom with Him, or will the lamp of your soul burn out before He comes? One way or the other, you will be involved in His return. No one will be left out.

If you are not living a life that's worthy of His bride, let Jesus come into your heart right now. Prepare yourself to enjoy the pleasure of His presence forever and ever. Be ready for the day when all the physical concerns of this life—including sex—will be no more. The joy of sex will end, but it will be replaced by the Lord's *"joy unspeakable and full of glory"* (1 Pet. 1:8). That joy can be yours.

## Notes

1. Harold Lindsell, *The World, the Flesh, and the Devil* (Washington, D.C.: Canon, 1974), pp. 110–11.

2. Ibid., pp. 216–17.

# My Challenge to You

If Jesus should come today, would you be ready? If you are not sure, I invite you to receive Jesus as your Savior now. You will be filled with hope and peace that only Jesus can offer.

Pray this prayer out loud.

"Dear Lord Jesus, I am a sinner. I do believe that you died and rose from the dead to save me from my sins. I want to be with you in heaven forever. God, forgive me of all my sins that I have committed against you. I here and now open my heart to you and ask you to come into my heart and life and be my personal Savior. Amen."

When you pray the Sinner's Prayer and mean it, He will come in instantly. You are now a child of God and you have been transferred from the devil's dominion to the kingdom of God.

Read 1 John 1:9 and Colossians 1:13.

—Lester Sumrall

# About the Author

Lester Sumrall (1913–1996), world-renowned pastor and evangelist, entered full-time service for God after experiencing what he recalls as the most dramatic and significant thing that ever happened to him.

At the age of 17 as he lay on a deathbed, suffering from tuberculosis, he received a vision: Suspended in midair to the right of his bed was a casket; on his left was a large open Bible. He heard these words: "Lester, which of these will you choose tonight?" He made his decision: He would preach the Gospel as long as he lived. When he awoke the next morning, he was completely healed.

Dr. Sumrall ministered in more than 100 countries of the world, including Soviet Siberia, Russia, Tibet, and China.

He established Feed the Hungry in 1987. In addition, he wrote over 130 books. His evangelistic association (LeSEA), headquartered in South Bend, Indiana, is still actively spreading God's Word. Dr. Sumrall's goal was to win 1,000,000 souls for the kingdom of God, and the ministry continues this vision. LeSEA ministry includes such outreaches as the World Harvest Bible College, radio and television stations, a teaching tape ministry, and numerous publications.

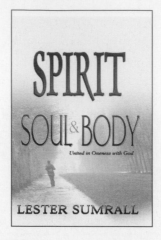

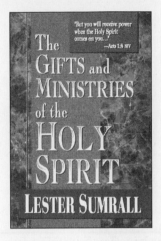

## The Gifts and Ministries of the Holy Spirit
*Lester Sumrall*

The gifts and ministries of the Holy Spirit function with
greatest accuracy through people who understand them.
This book defines the gifts and reveals their operations
in the body of Christ today. Discover how you can
operate in these gifts and be included in the great
outpouring of God's Spirit.

ISBN: 0-88368-236-2 • Pocket • 272 pages